Reflections

from a

Crop Circle Case

Valenya

Reflections from a Crop Circle Case

Dedication

3 people were so instrumental in the writing of this book, that it probably wouldn't have happened in the absence of any one of them.

My life-partner Terry de Lugo
Who held the fort (and booth), giving me the room and support, to chase the mystery both at home and abroad when I probably should have been at home making stock.

My brother Will Hirsch,
who relentlessly nudged me toward consciousness. Even to dropping the book Circular Evidence directly into my hands and demanding "Well? Explain this!" And I couldn't.

Which was written by

Colin Andrews,
Dean of Crop Circle studies and original trail cutter for so many of the crop circle 'pilgrims' who were eventually drawn onto the even larger mystery path through the weight of his work.

Acknowledgements

I would like to express my appreciation for everyone who contributed their accounts to this collection or helped in the gathering of them. You wrote the book!

This is literally true in the case of Kate Lawler who coauthored Kate's Story.

As well as Raymond Hunter who coauthored The Spectral Tree Stump.

I couldn't have put either story any better so I didn't even try.

I also want to offer a salute to those few others who also allowed me to use their real names. Takes a special and fearless person to stand behind an incredible account!

Special thanks to the staff of Fate, and especially to editor Phyllis Galde! Ever helpful and friendly, she allowed me to share my favorite discoveries with her readers through the agency of this timeless and classic Magazine. Many of the illustrations and certain accounts in this book were first run in Fate and were generously 'loaned' back to me for this book.

Special thanks also to Nancy Hayfield Birnes, editor of UFO Magazine, who encouraged me to explore subjects like UFO track lines (see end notes) and the crop circle mystery for their readers. Contributing work to UFO was quite a honor!

Thanks to those speakers at the Experiencers Speak Conference, 2014 who weighed in on my descriptions of their presentations to make corrections or suggest additions. Much appreciation to Nancy duTertre who went a step further, in offering me a free editing of the chapter as a whole. I believe she improved it.

Reflections from a Crop Circle Case

Certain stories (and illustrations) have been extracted, expanded upon and/or rewritten from articles previously appearing in Fate Magazine, especially Spirits of a different Shade, The Ghost of Mapleston Mine, Giant Salamanders times 2 and Besides Bigfoot.

The author would like to invite readers to share with her their own unusual experiences, through her e mail at vvalenya@yahoo.com

Valenya

"What's the strangest Thing that ever happened to You?"

When I first introduced crop circle jewelry into our Jewelry Booth at Craft Faires some 20 years ago, I noticed a certain number of customers tended to linger after examining them, as if they wanted to tell me something. Or they'd nibble around the subject of UFOs, while gauging me for a reaction. If I gave them the correct one, I'd be rewarded with a story. Often they'd wait until their mate/family had moved down to the next booth, far enough that they were out of earshot. And then they'd spill.

After a while I learned how to speed things up by asking them my favorite question. And it was always rewarding. First person accounts of UFOs, Ghosts and beings too strange to put a frame around. Of finding themselves in impossible situations with no memory of the lead in events.

Eventually, I even made up a line of ET Tee shirts to sell alongside my crop circle jewelry at UFO conferences, upping my odds of walk-by accounts even further. I suspect that the 'Experts' probably never hear some of the strangest stories. People are too in awe of them, afraid they'll think they're crazy. So they came to my table instead.

An extra benefit of T shirts was I could wear them myself, anywhere I went. Now people didn't even need to visit our booth. They'd see me coming a ways away, walk right up and start telling me things.

And living on the Yurok Reservation for twenty plus years, gave the T shirts a extra value. Wearing them about town, I picked up a lot of personal accounts concerning crypto-critters and UFOs that I never could have elsewhere.

Reflections
from a Crop Circle Case

Table of Contents

Part 1
Reflections from both Sides of the Case

Part 2
Reports from the Reservation

Part 3
House Calls and UFO Conferences

Valenya

Reflections

Part 1

Reflections from both sides of the Case

Everybody has a story, most folks more then one. Something astonishing that happened to them, that they never got over or understood.

And it's a story they want to tell, but they're afraid of what people, friends, family, co workers or bosses might think. Or call them. So they swallow it. But they still want to spill.

It was usually after I'd shown the customer a few crop circle pendants that I'd get 'that look'. Maybe I'd ask them my favorite question,--- "What's the strangest thing that ever happened to you?" if they seemed ready to engage. But you had to wait till they were or you could easily scare them away.

I remember one fellow, at the San Bernardino based Southern Renaissance Faire. A doctor, middle aged, prosperous looking fellow, who was enjoying the faire with his family. He noticed the crop circle designs, looked puzzled and asked me what they were.

As I told him about the crop circles and the various mysteries surrounding them, he started to get 'that look'.

"What do YOU think is making them?" he asked me, finally.

I told him that from what I knew, I'd rule out humans for many of them, we just didn't have the tech. Considering we're talking about removing subsoil water using a focused energy, that resembles microwaves in it's effects. Besides leaving a residual charge. Not done with two ropes and a board, at any rate.

Then he asked if I thought UFOs were responsible for those and I affirmed that I believed there could be a connection. His wife smiled tolerantly. These eccentric Faire Folk! She'd been listening to the exchange with amusement. The kids were turning restless. Time to move on.

The doctor had become quiet and now looked somewhat intense. But he continued down the road with his crew till they washed up at the air plants booth, about 100 feet away. And stopped to shop.

At that point, he couldn't take it anymore. He shot a desperate look my way, then started walking---fast!---right back to our booth. He was sneaking away from his family!

Before he'd even reached my crop circle case he informed me, loudly, that he'd seen a UFO, himself, once! And immediately proceeded to tell me all about it. It was a classic saucer, skimming low over suburban homes scenario. I suspect he'd probably never even told his family about it. Then, obviously relieved, he trotted off to rejoin them.

The stories my Crop Circle Case could tell! Fortunately the 'Case' standing behind it had pencil and paper at the ready under the counter, nestled with the price tags and change. No one ever rejected my request to take down or share their stories. At the same time, almost no one wanted their names revealed. I think you can understand why? It's nice to keep your job, your friends, your credibility?

For that reason, figure the names given are stand ins unless noted otherwise.

But the accounts are all real. You can tell by their lack of neatness, the loose ends, the baffling details. And that's what makes them so interesting---.

Crop Circles during the Renaissance

Generally, when you think of the English Renaissance crop circles are not the first images that come to mind. And one of the conditions for selling anything at the Renaissance Faire was that the object had to be tied in with England and with that particular period in history. No Australian boomerangs for example. No plastic kitch, no modern dress or Hopi jewelry designs.

I was already carving Anglo Saxon Runes into fossil tusk chips, and turning those into pendants, which was tolerated. People of that era still carried talisman and carved objects from bone.

But when I started carving crop circles on the chips, I wondered how I'd be able to find a historical connection in order to 'sell' them to our coordinators? Did they have crop circles way back then? And even if they did, how could I ever prove it?

Cerelia, the Grain Goddess must have smiled with amusement at my consternation. Soon after I'd started sneaking out my new wares, she provided me with all the proof I'd need.

Flipping through a crop circle book, I discovered an antique broadsheet printed during that era. Involving a Devil who 'harvested' a circle of grain. In order to punish a greedy farmer who refused to pay his workers, after they had already cut one of his fields, holding that they asked for too much.

"I'd sooner pay the Devil himself to cut my field!" he declared.

That night the sky lit up and was filled with strange and fearful noises. In the morning, a giant circle was discovered in one of the yet unharvested fields. Although the grain stalks were fallen, rather then cut, they were so magically intertwined that they could not be harvested. And so, the greedy farmer lost a great deal of his harvest.

Certainly a Mowing Devil had visited him during the night, to teach him not to cheat his laborers!

Underneath the story was a woodcut illustration of a 'Mowing Devil' complete with goat hoofs and horns, depicted merrily scything out a crop circle.

I copied the broadsheet onto parchment printer paper and hung it in our booth for validation of historic correctness. Our coordinators were not convinced but were overruled by the Faire's owner who turned out to have a lively interest in the phenomenon, herself!

The 'Game' evolved by accident. I think the first time I played it was when a young man gazing into the case mentioned that he was a musician. When he said that, I suddenly saw which pendant he was looking at. So I quietly reached in pulled it out, and handed it to him.

"How did you---?" he began.

"It must be your 'Glyph!" I answered. I wasn't just pitching, either. At that moment I was certain of it. And I guess he was impressed too, because he bought it.

Since that was so rewarding, I started doing it as a game. It was fun. I'm sure it made extra sales. And I think I truly united a lot of people with their personal designs over the years. Something I'd realized early on was that people tended to notice certain glyphs right away and be drawn to them alone, as though they recognized them as their personal medicine designs. I just provided extra validation.

Waking in the Foot-Well

A woman wakes up in her car, which is racing down the highway. She's sitting in the driver's seat, all alone, her hands tightly gripping a steering wheel, which resists her frantic attempts to turn it. Finally it yields and she directs the car into the next rest stop. Parks, turns off the ignition and collapses, shaking.

What just happened?

A psychologist might suggest sleep apnea. The woman's mind took a mini nap, then blinked back on, just before the crash could occur. Your local sheriff might inquire how much she'd had to drink? Or maybe sleep deprivation was the culprit.

Of course these answers only represent ABA (anything but alien) explanations. I'm sure you've heard of this classic UFO scenario before. Yet, to be reasonable, it's hard to totally dismiss the ABA answers completely, in the story set forth above. They are all plausible.

But what if just one aspect of the story was changed? What if the woman didn't wake up in the driver's seat?

One Saturday morning before the crowds had thickened two mid youngish fairgoers, a male and female, visited our booth. Sales were slow, the sun was warm so we spent some time chatting about puzzling subjects like crop circles. They seemed like good prospects, so I asked the female my favorite question. "What's the strangest thing that ever happened to you?"

She answered, without any hesitation.

"I woke up in my car." she replied. "In the foot well."

Strange? Well, maybe not so much. Must have been a pretty good party, though! I smiled, reflecting fondly on my own misspent youth.

But then she woke me up.

"And the car was going 40 miles an hour. Down the highway."

Recovering from shock, I asked her a stupid question. "How did you get in there?"

She didn't know.

Waking, in foggy confusion, to find herself packed tightly in the passengers foot well, she recovered her wits and scrambled out and across the seats, to slide into place on the driver's side. And be confronted with her next challenge, the infamous frozen steering wheel. Which finally gave in to her tugging and allowed her to take over control.

When I queried her concerning UFOs or aliens she looked puzzled. Now, why would I be asking her about anything like that? But no, no UFOs. That she could remember, anyway—?

At this point, her male friend interrupted. "I saw a UFO, once!" he informed me. A classic lenticular craft, it was sighted moving low and slow over his suburban neighborhood. Right over the rooftops. Everybody on his block saw it.

Normally, I'd be fascinated.

But his friend's story still had me baffled and I couldn't let it go.

Why would she wake up in the passenger foot well, of all places? And why didn't she remember seeing any UFOs?

What do you think? Here's a few of the possibilities I came up with.

The foot well---

Suppose you pull off the road to watch something strange, maybe colored flashing ariel lights, or the cover memory of a road crew makes you slow your car to a stop. Then you suddenly realize things are not as they appear and panic takes over. There is nowhere outside the car to hide. So you scrunch into the only available semi concealed spot you can find—the passenger's footwell—and hope they don't see you.

But they do, of course, and they take you anyway;--- so much for that plan. Do with you whatever they choose, then bring you back.

But, now—where to put you? Perhaps in the same spot they found you? In the same position? Maybe you would feel safer waking up in there, since that was where they found you hiding originally?

Of course, a person might reasonably argue, that the stress incurred by finding yourself congruently racing down the highway, might cancel out any such feelings of safety. Still, it might make some sense to an ET.

Now, what about the other part—her bafflement, "What UFOs?" One of our faire friends used to hold that there were probably UFOs passing overhead all the time. He figured that they were probably cloaked, as there would be no benefit in letting us know they were there. He suggested that if you saw one it was either malfunctioning or a decoy; meant to get your attention while the invisible one, hovering right behind you, beamed you up.

8

If she didn't see a UFO, maybe it was because it was simply functioning correctly.

Or maybe she had some help from the famous ET memory wipe?

Whatever took place, however, it probably wasn't a case of sleep apnea—

UFO Road Kill?

At North Faire in 96 I met a woman who didn't need to be asked about her most bizarre experience. She took one look at the crop circle pendants in the case and started right in.

Valenya

Emily was driving through the New Mexico desert late at night. It was 1986. She had one passenger, another woman.

At some point they became aware of a light in the sky, far ahead of them. It looked like a very bright star. But it was either growing larger or drawing closer to them; it was brightening rapidly. As they drove toward it, they also realized that it was "swinging back and forth" in the sky.

At this point, the women began to panic. Emily spotted an intersection not far ahead on the highway and she turned a full about face, speeding back in the direction they'd come.

But after only a few miles, they realized that the light had overtaken them, and was now swinging low in front of them. In fact it appeared to be landing on the highway directly ahead of their car.

Emily braked and swung the car around in the middle of the road. Again, they raced away to escape from the light.

Just as Emily turned the car the second time, she glimpsed a small dead animal lying on the side of the road. She didn't pay any attention to at that moment, being consumed by the need to escape.

But just a little ways down the road, the light caught up and passed them and once again, Emily braked to turn the car around.

And there was another dead animal laying by the side of the road. She couldn't make out what it was. It looked like a big hairy lump. It was about the size of a large dog.

Feeling no need to inspect it, she whipped the car around and headed away from the light. But before long it passed them overhead and once again began to land on the highway. By now both women were completely frantic.

As Emily swung the car around, yet once again, it's

headlights brushed the body of a very large animal lying on the side of the road. It was the size of a bear.

Their zig zag chase had led them to the very outskirts of their home town, and Emily gunned it. Once they'd entered town proper the light finally left them.

First Emily dropped off her friend. Then she went straight to see her grandfather, who was "a very skeptical man. He doesn't believe in God or anything." She wanted to collect him and then drive back the way they'd come, so he could see the craft for himself.

Although she retraced the very same roads she'd covered earlier, they couldn't catch a glimpse of either craft UFO or critters. One thing they did discover was an area of burned asphalt on the high way at one of the spots the craft was trying to land.

Emily says she took the same route less then a week later and found that the burned patch had already been cleaned up and the asphalt replaced.

So why the critters? Whether real or 'cover' images, you have to think they were placed there for a reason. But what could that be? Did they really think Emily would feel sorry for them and stop to see if she could help? Or that if small bodies didn't sufficiently arouse her compassion, maybe they just needed show her bigger ones? Baffling.

UFOs on Vacation

It's odd how many accounts I've gotten from folks who were on vacation at the time, especially in Europe. Maybe because that's the time when they're more likely to be outdoors, or lounging about near a window?

I met Lin at the South Faire in '96. A middle aged, confident looking woman, and an intelligent conversationalist, she looked like the perfect candidate to pose my favorite question to. I debated how to lead up to it, while she surveyed the display of crop circle pendants in the jewelry case. Then, with no prompting, she lifted her head. And told me she'd once seen a UFO.

It happened long ago when she was a kid and her f amily was vacationing in Spain. She was lying on her bed, in their rented apartment, reading a book that she'd felt compelled to buy earlier that day. Which was curious, considering she'd previously had no interest in the subject it covered. Then her Mom called her over to the window.

Hovering close to their apartment and directly over the beach, was a saucer shaped craft. It appeared to be made of silver metal, seamlessly connected. She didn't see any lights.

Down on the beach, below her window, she could see about 30 people all watching it as well. It traveled down the shoreline a bit, then suddenly blinked out. From metal to missing.

OK, that's interesting enough. But what are the odds that the book she'd been drawn to buy and was reading at the moment of her sighting, would be about UFOs? A set up by the ETs? Or a psychic premonition of her own?

Something I've often noticed with people who seem to be recalling a genuine sighting is that they tend to get a case of the jitters as they recount it. Sometimes their hands literally shake from the emotion. It's an exiting thing to recall. Lin was lightly shaking as she told me her story.

And the other 30+ people who saw the craft? Did they also experience baffling synchronicitys connected to their sightings? It makes you wonder---

Ivan was half of one of our favorite Faire couples. As often happens they started as customers, soon becoming friends and now often hung around our booth just to visit. I forget when I asked Ivan my favorite question, but he was certainly ready and waiting when I did.

It happened back in the late 60s or early 70s, when he was a young man. He was spending a vacation in France, renting a place on the beach. It was a warm day, but not crowded and he was enjoying the surf along with a number of other people.

He estimated that about one hundred other people witnessed the monstrous craft that appeared high over the beach. Not only was it huge, but it provided quite a show, in that it took it's time making it's entrance. And it appeared in a very strange manner,

At first, no one could tell exactly what was happening or what they were seeing. Because it was revealing itself slowly, beginning with the nose, and moving forward, bit by bit.

As he put it, "It was like it was coming out from behind a curtain."

Once fully exposed, it's size was boggling. And it wasn't alone, either; smaller lights swarmed around it like bees around a hive. The leviathan slowly moved along, following the shoreline, accompanied by the lights. Then the whole parade veered off to sea, finally disappearing into the horizon. For hours Ivan witnessed more lights emerge from the same 'curtain' area of sky, and follow the same path as the Mother ship, moving along the shore, then heading out to sea.

Of course you don't have to go overseas on vacation just to see a UFO. Or to not see one--- Mitchell not only didn't remember seeing any craft, he'd forgotten about the whole experience.

We were hanging the cloth ceiling to our jewelry booth, during pre faire set up and he offered to help. Handing us colored cloth wind flutterers to tie on poles, as we teetered on our ladders.

At this time Mitchell was working as head of field security at Faire. But we weren't opening for a few days still and he had some time left over on his lunch break. So he came by to help us set up. He was just that kind of guy.

And as he did so, he was entertaining us with stories of camping trips he'd gone on as a youth. Got talking about a canoe trip he'd taken all alone, somewhere back East, paddling far down a swampy river, laced with tributaries. It was too wet, remote and undeveloped to be accessed by any road so he'd figured it would be perfect for fishing. When he found a good wide shoreline, he pulled out the canoe, and hitched up his tent, far out of the mosquito range. Crawled in, hit the sack and fell right out.

Mitchell suddenly went silent. He stopped feeding me wind flutterers. I looked down at him. He was frowning.

"Dude!" he exclaimed, sounding astonished. He was staring inward and I paused in tying up the strips. Waiting for whatever revelation he'd obviously just experienced.

"All those kids?" he mused slowly. And then he explained.

Strangely, in spite of picking the most remote spot possible, and having met no one during the whole journey, in the middle of the night, the tent had lit up as if by a giant invisible searchlight, waking him instantly.
Illuminating the silhouettes of so many children against the walls of his tent, moving all around the area.

Then Mitchell paused again. I couldn't stand it and tried to nudge him forward.

"So, what happened next?" I suggested.

"I don't know". He admitted, sounding surprised about that as well. "I guess I must have fallen asleep?

But when I got up the next morning, there wasn't anyone there. But there were little tracks all over like kids would make. Except that the treads were weird; not flat, but rounded on the bottom.

But you know what's even stranger?" he asked me. "I just now remembered all of this! I'd totally forgot about those kids till now."

Mitchell grew silent again and resumed handing me cloth strips. I resumed tying them. Colored strips changed hands as both of us considered our similar experiences. He didn't know about mine. I'll get to those later.

I was also measuring him for my 'Cowbird Profile'; a casual research project I'd been lately working on. Which I'll also get around to further on in this book.

16

When Saucers Fumble?

Beth had a midnight job stuffing mailboxes. She was a young woman with a young person's energy and could easily handle a 10 pm to 5 am job without nodding out. Her route was out in the Arizona desert, the stuffage consisted of ranch news style periodicals. Being as the ranches were spaced at a good stretch from each other, she did more far more driving then stuffing.

She liked her job. She had a routine set up, the spots where she'd take a break. There was a green wild area with a small waterfall, about midway along her route. There, she'd drink some coffee, and eat a sandwich, throwing the crust to a coyote who was always waiting. It was a nice refresher.

While getting ready for work one night, Beth started feeling edgy and nervous. She didn't want to go, but she knew she needed to. So instead of enjoying the drive, she threw herself into it, focusing on just getting it over with as soon as possible.

Right from the beginning of her route, things felt wrong. If you've ever been in the desert at night, you know it's full of sound. Crickets, coyotes, owls---but nothing was calling tonight. Except for the sound of her car, total silence enfolded her as she drove along.

At her halfway point, it was still the same. Complete silence, and no coyote. Beth didn't finish her sandwich, but

17

got back in the car and ate as she drove. The silence continued. And the uncomfortable feeling of waiting.

By early morning, she moved into foothill country. Beth couldn't see far ahead in this area, due to the hills and rock formations, so she had to slow down. She didn't mind; once she'd hit this point, she was getting close to the end of her route. Then she rounded a hill and slammed on the breaks.

And stared at the mess strewn ahead of her, lying in the middle and the sides of the road; trying to make some sense of what she was seeing.

It was obviously a wreck of some kind. She debated as to whether she could detour around it, but realized that wouldn't be possible. In fact, she'd have to back her car for several miles, just to find a place on the road wide enough to turn around.

The police hadn't got there yet. Not surprising as it was

18

about 4 o'clock in the morning on a remote rural road. Did they even know yet?

Although she couldn't imagine the accident to be survivable, Beth parked her car and got out to take a look. The wreckage was that of a truck and cattle trailer. Only that. No other vehicles were around. That was strange, someone must have collided with it to cause such a mess. No other tire marks, no skid marks, nothing. Which seemed impossible considering that the impact suggested something at least the size of a semi. And then she realized something even stranger.

When something hits you, you bounce away from it. You don't bounce in every direction at once. And that's what seemed to have happened here.

Things don't fan out when you hit them, front on or from behind. But what if you were to drop them?

Because that's what it looked like. As if the truck and trailer had dropped from the sky and hit the ground.

Beth approached the cab of the truck. There was blood on the windshield. A man and woman were inside, obviously dead. They also looked as if they'd exploded outwards. Cattle were in the trailer, also dead.

At this point, Beth decided that her shift had just ended for the night. Some of the subscribers would just have to wait an extra day for the Cattleman's Gazette. As she'd figured, she had to back her car for miles, before turning around at an intersection. On the way home, she stopped at a pay phone and called the police, to report the accident.

That was the last night of her work week. She watched for news of the accident in the local paper, and on TV but nothing of the sort was mentioned. Before her weekend was over, she called the police to find out something about the accident. To be informed that she was mistaken; no accident

19

of that kind had taken place.

The first night of her next workweek felt normal. There was no foreboding, no silence, her coyote was back and eager for his handout. When she reached the place of the crash, she found that everything had been cleaned up.

I know Beth and she's a highly credible person; through intelligence, hard work and careful investment, she's made a good life for herself. So I didn't doubt her story. I just wondered what happened and what it meant?

Did the craft or whatever Beth was feeling all night decide to hijack the ranch couple instead of her? Maybe figuring to get cattle into the deal as well? But then the cattle started running about in the trailer, upsetting the balance and the craft fumbled it's cargo, dropping the whole package?

And what about the clean up? It's tempting to blame a covert secret security group, the NSA or CIA. But what if the ETs did it themselves, maybe trying to destroy the evidence before the police showed up? Might they have been hovering right behind the next hill, while Beth was inspecting the wreckage? Waiting for her to leave so they could finish loading up the vehicles and casualties and begin the scrub?

My Classic Abduction Report

You've probably heard this joke?
"You know, I think I was abducted by Aliens last night!"
"No kidding?!! Any strange scoops or markings?"
"Not really,--- just the usual---"

We've actually reached a point that a Classic Abduction motif has formed. It's funny; before, you were afraid your abduction story wouldn't believed. Now you're afraid it won't be believed if it doesn't fit the 'correct' pattern.

Of course, even if it does fit the norm, you have to still have to decide if it was good or bad? Pick your side. And the camps are deeply polarized concerning ET involvement. Mack and Hopkins summarized the rift. Agents for evolution or parasitic predators? Reminds me of Freud and Jung; how Freud's patients saw phallic symbols and Jung's saw Mandalas. I suspect different researchers may tend to collect the people and accounts they already agree with, consciously or not.

In contrast, the stories I've heard are so all over the map; in fact there's actually only one conscious report, that I've collected at Faire of that you might call classic. This one was so much so, in fact, that at first I didn't plan to include it as it seemed too 'normal'. But there were some interesting unexpected bits---

At last, an Abductee with troubled eyes! I'd read about those folks and even met one in my youth, but this was my very first since I'd begun collecting reports at the booth.

She was a young woman, in her twenties. I met her while she was visiting our friends on Faire site. Helping them to erect their booth pre Faire. We were building our own booth nearby, but it was time for a break. As we sat on the ground in a circle, to talk and eat lunch, she kept eyeing my EB Hybrid T shirt. When I announced that I was going to walk back to our booth, and collect some beers and sodas, she volunteered to help me. I wasn't surprised; that had actually been my plan.

Once we'd passed through the door-flap into into the back of the booth, she finally asked me about my shirt.

"Do you know them?"

I realized she meant that in a personal way, not in terms of research. So I replied that I believed I did know them and I'd had a connection with them for a very long time.

She relaxed. "So have I." she admitted.

Kim believed her whole family was involved. She believed she was being used as a breeder. During the last couple of years, memories had been surfacing.

Kim had eyes that could honestly be described as haunted. You could tell she had secrets that hurt and scared her to think about. Traumatic experiences that had left her in deep conflict.

At the same time, she appeared to be an intelligent person with a surprisingly quick if quirky sense of humor. I couldn't help measuring her for my Cowbird Chick profile. It was a good match.

Her last memory of an encounter took place in '93.

She found herself onboard a craft, accompanied by a tall and a short Gray. She recognized the short Gray from an earlier encounter.

"I remember you!" she exclaimed out loud and it seemed to smile in response. As if it was actually pleased that she did.

She didn't like it, though. It seemed too eager to tear into her, to see how she worked. "Curiosity without compassion", was how she put it.

She thought you could compare the tall one to the United Nations. It was there to insure that the small ones didn't harm her or go outside the limits of the 'Law'. She couldn't remember what was actually done to her.

Interesting that she recognized the small being rather then the tall. Usually, it's the reverse. In fact Smalls are often held to have no individuality, cloned meat robots. And the Talls are usually identified as doctors not diplomats. In this case it was a Small that was the doctor.

The fact that it smiled at her suggests a personality, or at least an ego.

She seemed open to discuss the idea of an Experiencer check list and interested in the concept and to find that she might fit the profile. The idea that there might be others like her, seemed to encourage her that there might be some positive element to the whole scenario that wasn't apparent at this point.

Watching her digest the idea, I was struck by the apparent contradiction, that people subjected to such baffling and intense experiences often seemed so evolved in attitude. I'd expect them to grow inward, becoming progressively more shaky and depressed. Yet, often as not, the challenge often seems to force growth.

The Loving Light Cone

Everyone, even nonbelievers, have fairly well defined ideas about what ghosts ought to look like. Ghosts are expected to be about human size and shaped. And although observable, they should be transparent to some degree and may even be so faint as to seem mist like. And everyone knows that ghosts are supposed to be scary; that's kind of their job description.

But could it be that this definition is no more then dogma canonized from generalities to create tidiness and uniformity? Because I have heard personal reports of ghosts that fit none of the 'qualifiers' listed above. I've always been fascinated by how many of these differ from the supposed spectral 'norm'.

Like this one.

Scott rounded the corner into his kitchen and there it was. Hanging in the air; a pyramid of light. And it was large. And sentient.

A cone shaped light? Might it have been some transitory phenomenon like a reflection through his windows? Maybe against a mirror or some such?, I wondered.

He insisted that there was no way it could have been a reflection.

"I could not see through the figure," he recalled, "and it was very bright; almost blindingly bright. It was triangular shaped, but taller then it was wide. My guess would be about 3' to 4' or so high, and 2' 6" or so wide.

From what I remember, it made me feel safe and I was not scared at all. It kind of had a calming effect, and made me feel like I was welcome and that it wanted me to see it. And I still feel that it was female and definitely not male in any sense.

I did speak to it but got no response and it seemed like we were 'looking' at each other for a good minute or two. I don't remember any facial or body characteristics but I felt like we were looking at each other.

But the thing I remember most was not having any fear. And when it vanished, it just disappeared. Not quickly, but not slowly. It is hard to explain."

I suspect it is. We may not even have the words in our vocabulary to describe the attributes and actions of such a being.

Was it really a ghost? If not, what? Although I've never heard of a cone shaped, light emitting, loving female spirit, even less have I heard of ETs matching such a description.

A few words on our friend Scott. A smart and forthright fellow, he develops architectural blueprints for school layouts for a living and hikes and fishes for pleasure. Probably not the person you might choose for "Most likely candidate for Bizarre Spirit Encounter"---but there you are. Normal intelligent people often see strange things.

Valenya

T Shirt Tales

The manager of the T shirt shop that printed up my EB Ts was a woman in her middle/late 30s. Short and energetic with cropped blond hair, she was a friendly person. I liked her right away. The way she hired local kids to do the work, even though having it out sourced overseas would have been way more profitable impressed me.

Pat kept tabs with us all along the process. We conferenced several times with her, before the work began as well as during and afterwards.

Once, while waiting to talk to her, I eavesdropped on two college age male workers who were setting up a silkscreen for my 'Annotated Alien' t shirt. Saucer in the background, In the foreground Ets were digging plant and soil samples in a desert somewhere. One was puzzling over a bottle cap labled Tree Toad Beer.

"The human one's not right." one kid remarked, pointing out a female in the background. "Her eyes are too big."

The other kid studied the template for a moment.

"It's probably a Hybrid." he informed the first one, and I smiled. And nudged Terry who also smiled. This was back in the early 90s, and the concept wasn't so well known.

Then they turned around to pick up stock and my jaw just about dropped. Should I be mad? I wasn't sure. Both of them were wearing shirts decorated front and back with my designs. Was this one of the perks of working here---free access to the customers personal silk screens?!

Then Pat walked in and caught me staring. She quickly explained that these shirts were trial proofs and rejects, those she let the kids keep, rather then toss them. I wasn't convinced; I wasn't printing any shirts with 2 sides covered. Then I noticed the paint slash across the front of each. Accidentally on purpose?---how careless of me; guess I'll just have to keep it! And print the back as well---

Once my irritation had subsided, I had to admit that they'd done a great job overall. We made arrangements to pick them up the next week when they were dry. But then she suggested we talk with her in her office before we left.

Her eyes had that familiar 'I have to tell somebody' look. We didn't even ask why, but followed her down a long rickety wooden hallway to a room at the very end. She sat down at her desk and we pulled up the two chairs stationed in front of it.

She began by telling us about a long, straight mountain chain called Friday Ridge, which was situated to the east of Eureka. Local people often saw UFOs moving overhead, as if using the line of the mountain range to sight their craft. She'd seen them herself, when she'd lived there.

When she saw that information didn't raise any eyebrows, she continued with the real stuff she'd wanted to talk about.

Pat was an experiencer, with more 'open' memories then about any I'd talked to thus far. Not only was she involved, but so was her husband---or at least since he'd married her. She believed that her whole family was involved at least as far back as her mother's generation.

She remembered how her mother would find her in her closet when she was a child. Pat would tell her that she'd been visiting her friends, the little blue people.

Later on, when she was older and living on Friday Ridge, she believed that she might have been involved again, though she couldn't remember any details.

She knew other people living on the Ridge that she'd suspected of being experiencers. Unlike her, however, they were more frightened by the UFOs then curious, even afraid the ETs might be demonic. So she didn't question them regarding their experiences. She never actually saw the forms of the craft, as the lights were too far away. But she could tell by their jerky movements, that they weren't made earth-side.

Mentally, I was starting to measure Pat for my Cowbird Profile. Kind nature, smart, new age sense of responsibility? Check. Curiosity about the unknown? Check. She seemed a very confident, upbeat person. Not by any means, a 'shattered' abductee.

I wished I could view her next to her parents to compare; taller or shorter?

Her images of the visitors themselves came mainly from dream fragments, teaching dreams. In one such fragment, people were sitting in a round, white room. They were undergoing training to receive and accept the energy of a blue light that was floating around their heads and shoulders. She said that the light was physically difficult to stand, without training.

The purpose of the light was to make them sensitive to each others thoughts. Essentially, they were being trained to be psychic. Pat mused that maybe the aliens didn't realize that humans consider their thoughts to be private, and prefer it that way. That sharing them, might be almost painful. Being as the ETs seemed to be hive beings, themselves.

But Pat had had some experiences that took place in waking time as well.

She woke up one night to find her husband shaking her and demanding to know where she'd been. She replied that she'd been asleep in bed all night, since she'd first gone to bed. But he insisted she'd been gone at least half of the night. He'd been searching for her for hours. Finally, he'd gone back to bed, himself, then woke up just a few moments ago to find her lying next to him.

Another time, he'd gotten up to use the bathroom and was shocked to find the ceiling was 'open' and he could see the stars right through it. As if it had simply evaporated. It took him a while to be able to put into words and explain to her what he'd seen when he got back to bed.

Pat told us about friends of hers that still lived on the Ridge who were into the 'Pleiadian thing'. According to information they'd received, the visitors are trying to ruin the monetary systems that the major world governments rely on, so they can't do any more damage. Towards the bankrupting of these financial bases, they're offering them Star Wars type technology.

They didn't specify how this ruination would come about, or how they'd gotten this information, so I mentally 'Gray-Filed' it under Interesting if True.

Pat had never undergone hypnosis, as she didn't feel damaged, emotionally or physically by her experiences.

We thanked her for the interesting information and headed back to the front desk to pay our bill. And to hear our next unrequested report.

Jan, the cashier, totaled our order and commiserated with us over the rising cost of t shirts. It was a slow morning, we were alone in the shop, and we chatted. She asked if the alien shirts were our own design. When we affirmed that they were and that we collected accounts, she jumped right in with an experience her husband had had.

He was out hunting with a buddy, in the hinterland Southeast of Eureka. They were far from human habitation, way out in hilly bushy country, when they spotted a large bright ball of light far to the west of them. It passed them directly overhead, moving at unbelievable speed. And continued on East.

Then they spotted another one, also originating in the West.

The reaction of the 2 men was interesting. Jan's husband was fascinated by the scenario and tried to make contact. As the second one passed overhead, he continued standing and even waved his arms about to get it's attention.

In contrast to his buddy, who, in reacting from shock and fear, had just collapsed behind a big rock. And was now energetically tugging at his friends pant legs, trying to get him to hunch down and hide with him. "Are you crazy?!" he hissed, in disbelief.

That was the whole show, though. The second light didn't slow down and there were no others following.

Jan struck me as a conservative young woman. The accent, the logger shirt, the country inflection. I figured she and her husband probably lived outside of Eureka.

And I thought of her husband, hunting far from town, almost alone, fearlessly trying to flag down a UFO. Couldn't help thinking that if and when contact was first made openly it would probably happen in this manner. One to one with those humans who displayed the least amount of panic. Way more functional then landing on the White House lawn, in any case.

I was feeling well satisfied and content with two fat fresh accounts as we left the t shirt shop. Multiple accounts volunteered by two people, brought about by my EB Ts--- and they weren't even out on the market yet!

Then we passed the kids with the pirated shirts, modeling them front and back.

Well, Hell, I thought. So let them 'steal' a few! I probably should even thank them. They were wearing the Annotated Alien and the UFO Expert designs, both of which had information 'bites' tucked in the corners; UFO types, ET races, theories etc. People will look at the shirts, ask them questions. They'll answer and information will spread. Wasn't that one of the reasons I'd designed them originally, after all?

Leaving the building, Terry remarked that maybe way more people were involved in initiating contact then were even aware of it. He didn't need to explain, I could tell what he was thinking.

Alien Home Bases?

Where do the UFOs come from and where do they go? We assume they come down from outer space, but could they have actually popped 'through' from another reality into our atmosphere at some point before we noticed them? And left the same way?

Because we've already heard about a blimp craft emerging from behind a curtain of 'sky' and a saucer blinking off. Is their 'home base' in outer or inner space? And if inner, where exactly is it? And what? Here's another 'blinker'.

What interested me was the attitude of the witness.

One customer, an older lady, well spoken, upper class, was telling me about a sighting she had experienced while visiting friends in San Francisco. They were indoors when they first noticed the saucer hovering over the house, so they didn't witness it's arrival.

At first, they watched it from inside the house. Moving from room to room, they peered at it through the windows. It moved slowly and silently overhead, it's body shining silver, blue and orange lights glowing from the bottom of the craft. At the time, she insisted, she felt no fear at all, but rather an almost religious awe.

When it had already passed over the house a number of times, they all ran out to get a good look. And then it blinked out. Just like the saucer in Spain.

In possible connection to this puzzle, a Faire friend, Jan, shared an experience she'd had, while lying unconscious for nearly a week, following heart surgery.

"The doctors said I was unconscious" she laughed. "But really I was completely awake the whole time. I just wasn't here."

According to Jan, she had spent that week sitting on a bench, sandwiched between her mother (dead) and an alien (live), of the Gray variety. They chatted the whole time. She greatly enjoyed the visit. I was frustrated that she couldn't recall exactly what it was they'd discussed.

At the end of the week, her mother told her that it was time for her to go back and she awoke from her coma.

Jan was adamant that her experience was very real, wherever it may have taken place. I suspect she was right. But I would have loved to know where it was that she'd spent that whole week? And what did they talk about?

Valenya

Slumming Pleiadians?

I first noticed them when they were still several booths down the road, meandering leisurely in our direction. They stood out from the rest of the crowd in a way I couldn't quite put my finger on.

Besides being remarkably attractive in a classic Nordic sense, they is. They looked like they could have been twins, brother and sister. Maybe in their mid thirties. They had an air of not caring, not worried. Something you notice with rich people and sometimes with artists.

My crop circle case was located at the area of the booth closest to the entrance of Faire, that year. So it was the first thing they saw and they stopped in front of it.

They quietly remarked on the crop circle designs between themselves, smiling. You could tell that they found the presence of such jewelry at such a Faire especially amusing.

In order to join the discussion, I initiated the game I liked to play with customers; 'Let me guess what piece you're looking at".

Without fanfare, I reached into the case and picked up the piece I 'saw' them both looking at and handed it to the woman.

"That's right." the man noted, as his companion admired the piece. "What can you tell me about it?" Smiling like he had a joke he wasn't sharing.

I was a little thrown off by his utter non reaction. Like what I'd just done was only to be expected. There were well over 30 pendants in that case! Still I related the history of that particular crop circle I'd engraved on the fossil chip.

The female handed it back to me. The male leaned over the case.

"What about that one?" he asked. He didn't point but merely gazed through the glass in an unfocused way.

I could 'see' the piece he wanted so clearly. Too clearly, too easily. Way too easily-!

36

At last, it was my turn to be shocked. He not only knew I was playing 'the game' but he'd decided to play it with me. And he was way better at it then I was. Moreover, from the conspiratorial way the two continued to smile at each other, it was obvious they were in it together.

Since I could mentally see the piece, I pulled it out and handed it to them. I realized that it wasn't a case of me reading their thoughts, as of them shooting them at me. I'd become the passive partner.

In all, I probably pulled out about 6 or 7 pendants which they 'selected.' I didn't get one wrong. And I gave them the histories concerning each Glyph, although I had a nagging suspicion that they knew more about the phenomenon then I. They were just curious to see how much of it I had right. It was entertaining for them.

I felt so thrown off by the situation that I was having trouble thinking, while it was happening, although I was somewhat aware of how bizarre this situation was. It never really struck me full force until after they'd left.

They lingered for maybe a half hour. Finally the male said he had one more question for me.

"What was your face before you were born?" he asked.

I'd heard the question before, thought it might be a zen koan. I could only answer honestly, that I could not imagine a time when I didn't exist.

They liked that. "Good answer." he replied. Then they laughed and thanked me for all the time I'd spent 'educating' them.

"I shall see thee on the rebound!" I remarked with a smile, as they turned to leave. A joke, it inferred that the road hit a dead end not far past our booth and they'd have to turn around and pass us once more on their way out.

37

They never looked at any of the other cases in our booth, but headed straight down the road. After they'd left, I shook off my inertia, realizing that something strange and exiting had just taken place. I wanted to tell the others at the booth. I realized that none of them had caught the interchange. But I didn't know how to start and everyone was currently engaged with customers.

So, instead, I watched for my visitors to return and pass the booth, going the other direction. But they never did.

I've heard that some ETs look enough like us to pass as human and I suspect they probably go Earthside, sometimes, if only for a lark. And I'd always entertained the possibility, that some day one might visit me at the booth at Faire. With everyone in costumes, it would probably be the easiest place to go unnoticed. I'd been mentally asking for such a thing to occur for years, in fact. But when it finally did, I didn't even recognize it until it was all over.

Cowbird Chicks Part 1

A couple times of times already, I've mentioned a profile I've been compiling over the years, establishing certain consistent areas of 'overlap' among UFO Experiencers. Because it was obvious that they existed. I might as well have made up a check list.

One common trait was a sense of humor and a perspective for the 'big picture'. When Mitchell opted to spend his lunch hour helping us put up the booth, that would have been right in line. Or when he spent his ostensibly free after hours hunting down faire kids who'd wandered off from their designated pack, which he often did, as well.

An expanded sense of responsibility was also evident in Pat's choice of business options. Choosing to employ local youngsters at the expense of loosing a bigger profit by not out sourcing would be consistent.

They seemed to be relatively intelligent compared to humans as a herd. They also tended to be psychic and they often had stories of ghost encounters along with those of ETs.

When I could view possible Experiencers lined up alongside their families, (which I did often at booth,) I also started noticing certain physical characteristics. For example, many were noticeably taller then their family, (although, oddly, about a quarter of the time, they were quite a bit shorter; the group to which I would belong). And often as not more attractive as well.

At first I wondered if ETs might simply be drawn to this sort of person. After all, if you plan to invest in a person for whatever reason, you probably want to pick one that will survive and thrive. Humans who look good and are tall, get treated better, and deferred to more. Statistically, it's just a fact. And it's also probably smart to pick psychic humans, if you look at it as an edge.

Nowadays, I wonder if I was just scratching the first layer of the agenda? Maybe those qualities were not so much an attraction for the ETs as features they've been embedding and upgrading in our species for a very long time.

This greatly disturbed Bud Hopkins and continues to worry David Jacobs but I think they may be getting things askew. There's a richer agenda then the one they're afraid of.

I like to use the term Cowbird Chicks to describe this aspect of what may be going on, but in language colored from the human, fear based viewpoint. It's a somewhat ironic term but there's a few reasonable parallels.

You've heard of Cowbirds? They can't raise their own chicks so they lay their eggs in the nests of other birds. Who greatly value their chicks for being larger then their own and nurture them accordingly.

OK, that sounds troubling, right? Hybrids slipped into a human nest? Well---maybe that's not exactly the story.

Yes, we're different from the herd at large but in beneficial ways, at least from what I can see. We will be different beings in the future then we are today as well; that's just called evolution. We don't shoot our kids to ensure that evolution doesn't continue. We accept it, welcome it, some of us even hope it would kick up a notch, we could use it right now. Maybe this is exactly what's going on, moving us into Fast Forward? A sneaky upgrade?

I'm not persuaded these are ET genes being adding to the mix, by the way. I suspect genes harvested from our own great great grandchildren would be a much better fit then ETs, and might accomplish the same ends. Although ETs may well be behind the mechanics, the test tubes and time travel? Are we being hybridized with our own future? Perhaps even with our own personal descendants?

When you read the reports following, consider how the intelligences behind the events often seem to know what we're about to do long before we get there---even years ahead--- and even set the stage for us beforehand? How else could they do this, if they couldn't move through time? When a UFO 'winks' out is it actually traveling into the future or past?

For them moving through time may be as easy as moving through space.

Reflections from a Crop Circle Case

Part 2

Reports from the Reservation

For thirty plus years we resided on the Yurok Reservation in Northern California. Our neighbors were a mixture of native people, Yurok, Karuk and Hupa, and white people; loggers and more recent arrivals from 'down under'--- meaning anywhere more then 50 miles south of the reservation.

Most of the following reports were essentially given over the back fence, by our closest neighbors. And it seemed like everyone had seen something strange in their own back forty at one time or another. Bigfoot being the best known, but also UFOs and some lesser known cryptids such as George--- the little monster I saw myself.

BigFoot in our Back 40

Back in 1977, when we were in our late twenties, Terry and I moved to a remote mountainous area on the Klamath River. Our property was located on the Yurok Reservation, which adjoins the Hoopa Reservation to the South and the Karuk Traditional lands to the East.

As we discovered later, we were also living only two miles away from Bluff Creek, celebrated for the Patterson video, and the striding buxom lady Bigfoot.

We heard some loggers laugh about the tracks they made for the newspaper reporters back in the 60s and 70s. But during the same time period, full 55 gallon drums of fuel were being tossed about the logging camps during the night, as lightly as if they were tin cans. And someone was leaving the logging area peppered with giant footprints. In any case the tracks were being found in this area long before the white people showed up. As well as the beings who made them.

And it wasn't even as though there was only one kind of Bigfoot either. Because, going by local Native tradition, it sounds as though there were at least three different varieties.

Ivan Sanderson, classic Cryptozoologist, noted this himself long ago, having studied our particular area in depth.

And In 'To the American Indian', a book written at the turn of the nineteenth century by Che Na Wich A Wa, aka Lucy Thompson, a local lady of the priestly Talth clan, these distinctions are described.

The giant Ridgewalkers lived high on the mountaintops, traveling along the ridges. Those Bigfoot you didn't want to meet. They were brutish and cannibalistic. And huge, up to fifteen feet tall. Since the Yurok used the river for transportation, they didn't bump into Ridgewalkers very often.

Then there was the type most commonly reported these days, as well as then, smaller in size, maybe eight foot tall but more likely six or seven. Thick bodied and usually covered in black or reddish hair, they lived in the middle elevations and you might meet them out hunting. Also called the Rock People for their habit of smearing their fur in conifer pitch, then rolling in gravel. Much more reasonable then the Ridge-walkers; If you met one on the trail, you would both probably back carefully away.

According to a local waitress in a Hoopa Cafe (best acorn soup!) these smaller forms of Bigfoot should be regarded as Forest Protectors. Terry had just told her that I was collecting reports about Bigfoot and UFOs. So she chose to spend her next break at his table and educate him a little.

She began by telling him about a good place in the area to watch for UFOs, a small community closer to the coast that I was soon to hear about again from other sources.

And she told him that unless he was seen as a threat to the forest, Terry didn't need to worry about the 'smaller' form of Bigfoot. It was the Little-foot you really had to watch out for!

Smart and mischievous, small and slender, the Little-foot resembles a fur covered 8 year old child. It only lives in the narrow band of Redwoods that runs along the coastline, inhabiting areas of dense cover and precipitous landscape.

Unlike the shy larger form of Bigfoot, the Little-foot delights in being glimpsed by Humans. It entices them to chase it into the deep woods, moving just slowly enough to where they believe they can catch it. Leading them into the densest, most confusing patch of forest it can find, until they're utterly lost. And then it sneaks away.

We were privileged to meet the last recognized Indian Doctor of the area, Calvin Rube, shortly before he passed. A highly respected person locally, he once remarked to Ivan Sanderson that he'd often wondered how long it would take the White People to catch on to the presence of Bigfoot?

Little-foot

Valenya

One first hand report I collected of a Bigfoot, from the Orleans area near Bluff Creek, was not of a sighting, but rather of a smelling. Bigfoot are notorious for rank B.O.

A young white man related an experience to us of some years past that occurred to him while climbing a foot-trail with a friend in the National Park. It wound along the steep side of a mountain.

Above them, they could make out a flat staging area/resting spot with a high stone wall surrounding it. As they climbed the stony ground, nearing the flat, they became quickly aware of a foul smell, which got worse as they continued. At the same time, they were both becoming increasingly uneasy. Finally, they reached the flat. And there, just behind the wall, sunken in the soft dirt, were the tracks. And the place really stunk. Judging from the direction the tracks were pointing, it had been watching them approach on the trail below.

Bigfoot are often held to have a supernatural aspect. You read of people shooting them, with no effect. Unless they disappear on the spot. Some people believe that though physically real, they have the ability to go through dimensions. Maybe this makes sense of this next account. Or not?

We had a Native Hupa friend who liked to go 4 wheeling at night, on mountainous snow covered logging roads, to the west of the reservation. One such night, around the Christmas season, with a big full moon to light his trail, John felt the urge to drive for a spell. High on a ridge road, he found a wide spot to park his truck, intending to stretch his legs. There was plenty of light to see by. That's when he noticed the big tracks crossing the road, not far ahead of his truck.

47

He stood next to them, comparing them to his own. The prints seemed about 3 to 4 inches longer then his foot in a boot. The toes were exactly like a human's and well defined. What he found especially interesting was the depth of the tracks.

There had been two hard snows recently and the snow level was deep. The recent top layer was soft and fluffy but the older bottom layer from the earlier snowfall had melted and refrozen into a hard crust, dense enough for him to walk over. So he followed the tracks, which had broken through both layers.

He knew what it had to be. He knew bear tracks and these were not those. They led him across the road. And then they vanished.

Although there was plenty of cover in the way of tall trees on both sides of the road, there was still a thick crust of snow covering the ground underneath the canopy. There should have been tracks.

John noticed a strong unpleasant yeasty smell in the air, which suggested that the Bigfoot had only recently crossed the road. He also discovered some scat that looked different from any forest animal he knew. And he was familiar with all of them. The size and shape he compared to a can of tomato paste, cylindrical but relatively short. Later he went back to get photos of it, which he offered to show us.

Sitting with us at our kitchen table, we debated what the vanishing tracks might suggest? He proposed that Bigfoot being an ape, perhaps he'd simply swung up into the closest tree and then traveled from one to the other? He pointed out that the tracks started and ended right at the tree line. The trees were Redwood and older growth fir, tall and wide. The branches were pretty stout. Maybe they preferred to travel from tree to tree and that's why their tracks were seldom found.

I don't know. Would even a redwood limb hold such a huge being? I'd also heard of them disappearing in plain view. But his theory did make sense in the old growth forest zones; wider limbs, stronger trees. Could the loss of their original highway system, through logging, have helped diminish their range?

Maybe Bigfoot researchers should stick to those areas of old growth for best results. And it might not hurt if they were looking up sometimes instead of just straight ahead?

Whatever Bigfoot are they behave a lot like normal forest beings in most ways. John later discovered from reading the weekly local paper, that on the same night he found those tracks, another man had also gone out for a drive. In this case, in order to carry a pickup load of garbage to the dump. The Hoopa dump is located out of town, in the woods and tends to be frequented by bears. As he drove into the parking lot, he could see something big rooting around in the big metal container. Not being in a hurry, he settled into his seat to wait it out. Finally a massive form crawled out of the dumpster, rose up on it's hind feet and ran away – on two legs.

And besides Bigfoot---

It's funny that the area we lived in is famous for Bigfoot sightings, yet so many other mysterious creatures have always shared the area with the local Native People while remaining more or less unknown to those outside the reservation. There's a River Serpent called a Kamas, with a body "as round and wide as a barrel" to quote a neighbor. It liked to wait in the river for unwary swimmers, then drag them down to it's house of stones on the river floor. Not only Native people way back when saw them, either. Our neighbors, prosperous well regarded white people, long established 'on the river', told us about a sighting one of their relatives had made of a Kamas, traveling in an undulating motion along the surface of the river. The witness estimated it's length at about 30'. The Klamath is host to giant sturgeon, but they are bottom feeders and move from side to side.

You weren't safe from strange creatures on land either, it sounds like. Parents used to keep their kids from wandering off at night by telling them stories about the Fog Devils. These hid in the thick tide of mist that rolled in in the Evening. Only the red lights of their eyes gave them away, burning through the haze. They looked for children and young women to kidnap.

Kidnap? Or abduct? Today, colored lights moving in an

enveloping mist, looking for humans to grab, hints at another interpretation besides Devils.

The same neighbors who told us about the Kamas also had heard about some other beings, sounding something like malevolent elves, that lived across the river in an old mine of some kind. You didn't want to meet them either.

But long ago there were some beings you'd be happy to

meet on the trail. They were wise and kind and literally glowed. The Yurok people discovered them already living in the area, when they first arrived.

According to Yurok tradition, their tribe was coming to the end of a very long migration, which began far to the East. The fact that their language seems to be a dialect of Algonquin supports this.

Lucy Thomson (Chee Na Wah Weitch ah wah) the Priest-clan Talth woman of the Yurok tribe related that the people her tribe encountered at the end of their migration had lived in the area a very long time and were not exactly human. They were called Wagas, meaning shining people. Generous and friendly, they welcomed the Yurok and invited them to join them, settling on the river alongside their own homes.

Their morals were very high, inspiring the same standards in their new neighbors. They taught the Yurok people many useful arts, living peacefully together, and at times intermarrying. After some time, however, the Wagas informed the Yurok that it was time for them to leave, returning to their original home to the north. Some say they actually went up into the sky. But before they left, they promised to return someday.

The Yurok were saddened to see them depart. They took along with them all of those children of half Waga blood or more, but left those with less then half behind with their Yurok relatives. These children did not shine but were said to be noticeably lighter in color then full blood Yuroks.

An unfortunate consequence of the word Waga--- the word meant white as well as shiny. This led to a disastrous misunderstanding when the white people first arrived, many centuries later. At first they were warmly welcomed, as long lost friends. That illusion soon crumbled as a measles epidemic wiped out some 50% of the Yurok people within the first two years of contact. Followed by murder and land theft, the usual story.

According to Thomson, during her lifetime, some people still awaited the return of the real Waga.

But remember, they never entirely left! Their DNA still remains among the Yurok in their mixed blood grandchildren. Probably much diluted, but again, maybe not? Lucy Thomson belonged to the Priestly clan called the Talth, as earlier noted. And she tells us something about them. They were different from other people, smarter, more adroit. They liked to marry within their own ranks. During ceremonies, they walked separate trails then the other people. They were expected to set an example for the others.

Are the Talth the descendants of the Waga? It's not hard to imagine the children of the the Waga stepping in as leaders, once their parents had left. And, over time, becoming a separate class of their own. Wouldn't you expect a Talth Elder like Thomson to take up the responsibility of compiling and publishing a history of her people, so knowledge of their traditions would not be lost?

Over the Back Fence

Marion was our next door neighbor and one of the first white women to raise her family so far down the river road from Weichpec. In the 60s the county 'highway' of 169 was still essentially a one lane, dirt logging road, only used by locals. Her husband Saul was a logger and her 6 kids attended a one room schoolhouse, where they were the only non Native pupils. They lived on a large flat about a mile above the Klamath river.

Many of their kids had remained on their land, to build their homes and raise their families. Probably making Hibber's ranch the largest community west of Weichpec till you reached 'End-of-the-Road' some 14 miles further down. The land was remote and still completely wild when we first moved onto the mountain. All roads but the highway were still unpaved. Giant logging tracts surrounded the Hibber's Ranch, eventually hitting Forestry land, mostly all of it densely covered in 2nd generation fir.

A well grounded and sensible woman, Marion once surprised Terry and I by recounting an experience some friends of hers from Eureka had had while attempting to visit her. They were ready for the bad roads but weren't prepared for the roadblocks---

Valenya

The quickest way to get to the Reservation from the coast was by taking the Bald Hills road, a dirt road which was just wide enough to pass someone else---sometimes. Although a little steep in places (think scenic!) and wilderness from beginning to end, it was quicker then taking the looping highway further east that ran through Hoopa. But you could lose your way under a light cover of snow, or slither off in wet weather and it was still a good 2 hours drive from the turnoff on 101 to Marion's place.

Marion's friends were just about an hour into their journey. The meandering road had passed through the coastal redwood area, and was now climbing the Bald Hills. Less trees up here, you were essentially driving along the ridge, occasionally cutting through high grassy valleys.

They were just coming out of a turn and entering a small meadow when they saw it. Not far ahead, mid meadow, in fact, and just off to the side of the road stood a large silver sphere. Standing up off the ground, propped on some sort of metallic legs.

At first, their curiosity propelled them forward, although they slowed down as they did so, in order to see it better. Then panic took over and they swung the car around, exiting the meadow and racing home. They never came out to visit again. The reason Marion laughed was that they seemed to blame her for it. The way they told her later what had happened, you would have thought it was her doing.

She said she had another friend who simply refused to drive the Bald Hills at all, because of the lights she saw in the sky; she said they made her feel creepy.

Those little lights! Marion told us about a brother of Saul whose family lived along the Klamath on the northern side of the Bald Hills. They enjoyed sitting outside in their lawn chairs on warm nights and watching the lights that wiggled and jumped around in the sky.

And they encouraged any overnight guests to join them, especially the skeptical ones. The display usually made such guests extremely nervous, to their hosts great amusement. I was a little surprised that Saul's brothers family wasn't a little concerned, themselves? Living right beneath all this? I guess you can get used to anything if it doesn't hurt you. I've also noticed it takes a bit more to scare mountain people.

One of Marion's daughters Anne told me about an unsettling experience she'd had as a young woman while walking alone at night down on the Klamath river bar at Knotchko. It was easier to walk alongside the river then through the woods above the river bank. The only problem with that idea was that other critters like mountain lions and bears often thought along the same lines.

But those weren't what she met. Instead, with no warning and less noise, a blindingly bright tunnel of light shot down from the sky above; like a giant spotlight. Bathing the earth all around her, illuminating the rocks and driftwood at her feet.

Shooting down----but from where? Anne saw no object above it. It just seemed to originate from somewhere in the sky.

Startled, Anne understandably panicked and ran away from the river bar, fleeing uphill and into the cover of the woods. She saw the searchlight sweeping the area behind her, but it must not have been chasing her or perhaps hadn't even noticed her because it didn't directly follow her but slowly swept the area. She headed for and hid inside the ruin of an abandoned cabin, which was covered by a clump of trees from arial view. And she watched from the windows of her shelter, as the spotlight reached the cabin and swept the ground outside. Finally it moved out of her eyeshot and she snuck home.

Marion's daughter in law, Cindy, is Native and her mother and grandmother live upriver in the Orleans area. During the 70s both of them witnessed a large bright red globe of light down close to the river, just skimming the treetops, slowly moving west. It seemed to be following the river valley, heading out to the coast. Their accounts agreed with each other completely. Which is surprising, considering that the women actually made 2 separate sightings, witnessing the object exactly a year apart! Cindy made a special point about this.

Giant Salamanders I have Known

OK, I admit it, there was really only one; my friends, relatives and neighbors saw the others. But it makes you wonder. After the other traditional monsters I've described that no one's ever heard about, is it really surprising that such a crypto critter as this one could exist up to the present day in our own back yard without science having a clue as to it's existence?

During our first years on the mountain, I used to go out on solo hiking and camping trips; overnighters, exploring old logging trails. I carried a hammock, and flashlight, and brought a rifle for protection. I'd never seen a mountain lion, though I knew they were out there. And although we had no shortage of black bears, they were shy and ran at loud noises. Still, I usually only rested during the night; too alert to sleep. Listening.

On this particular night, I hung my hammock just off a critter trail, which led downhill to a small creeklet. It was late Summer or early Fall and the leaves were starting to fall and dry up.

When anything stepped on them they crunched. And the madrone trees were exfoliating and crackling as they shed their bark. Wild termites scritched as they dug into rotting wood. Occasionally I'd flip on my flashlight to expose a squirrel that sounded as big as a badger.

Sometime, around early early morning, I heard something approaching from above, slowly crunching down the critter trail. It sounded big and heavy, scuffling as it came. It was heading straight toward me.

I swung out of the hammock and dropped onto the ground. Picked up my rifle and clicked on the flashlight. Then I set the rifle against a tree and stared in shock.

My first thought was that it had to be a dinosaur. Some relic species? It was about three feet long, heavy and cumbersome looking. And it seemed frozen by the flashlight beam, opening and closing a huge mouth, it's tiny inset eyes blinking.

Then I realized it had to be a salamander, but not like any I'd ever seen before. It seemed so primitive. Even the so called Pacific Giant (12" max.) has a round, pretty head, a gracile body, big round eyes. In contrast this thing was heavy bodied and flattened, the head as well. And it's eyes were inset and tiny. It's patterning was bizarre and colorful, splattered orange-yellow over black or maybe the other way around. Low and lumbering, it certainly wasn't built for a quick get a way.

I actually considered untying my hammock and netting it to wrap and carry home. I doubted any one would ever believe me otherwise. It didn't look like it could hurt me if it couldn't bite me. But to get home I'd have to jump a wide deeply set creek that I could barely manage as it was by myself. Certainly not with a heavy wiggling amphibian held in front of me. And it looked like it could weigh upwards of ten pounds or more.

I'd tied my hammock safely well above it's reach, so I climbed back in, hung the rifle on a branch and turned off the flashlight. What else could I do? At least I knew I'd seen it, whatever anyone else believed.

And I listened to it pass, waddling on on down to the creek.

That was back in the mid eighties.

It took me years to share that experience with my neighbors. When I finally did, I wished I'd done it long ago; they had stories of their own!

Our closest neighbor, living about a mile away, opened her front door one morning to find an identical salamander occupying her porch. Thinking her kids were playing a joke on her, probably an inflatable toy, she smiled; it was the sort of thing they'd do. "But then it moved and I screamed!" She recalled, laughing. Retreating inside, she'd waited till it was gone.

She lived with her large family in a sprawling hand-built house, situated on a fern and berry vine covered flat, next to a creek. Lots of nice damp protective cover underneath. It occurred to me that this big boy might have lived under there for years already before she spotted it. And maybe years after as well.

My second closest account in terms of proximity was given to Terry by her Native American son in law, who lived about a block away from her. Terry had told him I was collecting reports of giant salamanders and he didn't sound at all surprised when Terry described them.

"Yeah, I've seen them", he allowed. "But I don't bother with any that are less then a foot and a half long. Not enough meat on them." A disturbing picture. Is that how they became so rare? Big, tasty and slow moving.

The third closest account came from a friend living about five miles upriver from us.

He also lives on a lushly forested piece of land with a creek running through. It was Summer, midday and he was involved in moving a pile of firewood from one spot to another. Underneath the very bottom layer of wood-chunks, he discovered two giant salamanders.

"What the Hell IS that!?" He remembered thinking. Like me, it took a moment for him to figure out what they were.

He estimated their sizes as about two feet. And at least five pounds apiece. He remembered needing both hands to move each one away from the danger zone, so they wouldn't risk being crushed.

He remembered the markings, especially. "Not spots!" he emphasized. But ringlets, white on one, light yellow on the other. Delicate ringlets over a base color of dark brown. He wondered if the difference in color might suggest two sexes were represented?

I showed him photos of large salamanders of North America I'd been collecting for comparison. He thought it might have been a form of Tiger Salamander. One problem with that is that nearly all Tigers live in the Eastern United States, and none in Northern Cal. Also none of the subspecies grow to more then one foot in length. And no ringlets.

Or so I thought at the time. Since then, I uncovered a mini Tiger, the California Tiger Salamander, which survives as a tiny relic population in mid-state California. It has ringlets. But it also grows no longer then 6".

Much like our friend, I'd been leaning toward the possibility of an unrecognized relic group surviving in our area. And the Tiger did look to be it's the closest relative. The tiny eyes, the flattened body and the patterning were identical, only expanded. Salamanders are notorious for relic groups, backed into narrow environmental niches, and such groups are still being discovered. Researching Tiger Salamanders, I was not surprised to find that they spend nearly their whole lives under deep leafmold, beneath fallen trees, or in holes in the ground.

They only come out during the breeding season, to visit the closest boggy water source, and spawn. Usually that's during in monsoon season, Fall, early Winter, out here. Not a time many people would be sloshing through forest swamps in high mountains. Even a monster salamander could go unnoticed, hiding among the still massive second growth conifers, with a forest floor covered by huge rotting fallen trees and intermittent marsh.

And it wasn't only on the Yurok reservation that I heard the stories, but so far westward that they nearly ran into the beach. Encouraged by the reports I'd heard, I started telling my story further afield. I told my brothers family my story. Then they told me theirs.

Will, wife Lin and sons Ken and Evan all saw it. Lin verbally gave me the report while the others filled it in.

It happened during a camping trip in Mill Creek Campground, located near Orick, California. Orick is another very damp area, filled with ferns and forest and set right on the coast. Lin and Will were relaxing in camp chairs, reading, while the kids explored the local surroundings; the plants, rocks and occupants underneath.

Suddenly they burst into the campsite, demanding that their parents come with them to see the 'big lizard'. Will and Lin tried to beg off, but they insisted. So they got up and followed them to the farthest, situated in the marshiest part of the campground, under deep forest shadow and through mushy brush. Curled inside a giant hollow redwood stump was a giant salamander about three feet long.

Although it seemed aware of them, it didn't look like it wanted to escape, or that it could even move fast enough to do so if it tried.

It was squat and wide, avocado green in color, with markings that were slightly lighter. Will recalls that it hissed at them.

When two siblings see the same unknown being in places some thirty miles apart, as Will observed, "It really makes you wonder how rare this critter actually is?"

I wonder how many other people may have seen it but not reported it, because who would you tell? Unlike Bigfoot there's no frame or precedent to qualify such a sighting. At least many other people have reported seeing Bigfoot.

Why the color difference? I referred to my Salamander book, to discover that among Tiger salamanders, mountain subspecies tend to be brighter marked, coastal varieties more dark and drab. Maybe this also accounts for George. Yep, somebody actually named one.

About ten years ago during a visit to our dentist, and friend, Greg Mellon in his Mckinleyville clinic, I was recalling my run in with the giant salamander. When I'd finished my story Greg turned quiet. But instead of snickering, he murmured thoughtfully, "A giant salamander, hmm? Valenya, I saw a giant salamander myself!"

It happened on a warm summer morning in 1987 while he was wiggling along underneath his house, dragging a cable he intended to install. This house, for the record, located yet once again, in a swampy area, close to a creek. Moving slowly, on his belly, in the crawl space, he suddenly came face to face with a salamander he estimated to be between two and a half to three feet in length.

It was parked behind a pier block in the darkest farthest area from where he'd wiggled in. Greg managed to pull a rapid reverse and wiggled away backwards.

"I was blown away!" he recalled. "It looked like a Komodo Dragon!" It's head was well defined, it's body had more of a raised mid-ridge over it's spine then the one I'd seen. It was also darker brown, without spots, but then again, it was found near the ocean.

Years later, Greg happened to be talking with the person who had sold him his house. And he asked him point blank if he'd known there was a giant salamander living beneath it.

His friend just laughed, shrugging it off. "Oh, so you met George!" he replied. He'd named it. As Greg observed, "He had a relationship with it!"

An interesting postscript to this pile of salamander sightings came in the form of a supposed local Native American tradition, which gives our little monster a different name.

Some years after my sighting, I checked out a book about Bigfoot from the local library in Willow Creek. It was amateur writing and a rather thin book, but bulked up at the end for filler with other semi related local Native stories and legends. And the next to last chapter concerned the Poof Poof.

The chapter was titled The Monster of the Siskiyous, but the physical description perfectly fit my Humboldt monster, both in size and pattern. And it was known as a Poof Poof. Poof Poof liked to cache his acorns in the woods in conical pyramids. If you saw one, you'd know you were near his home. And you never ever stole his acorns! Because although Poof Poof was said to be very ugly, even fearfully so, it was also very honest and was always a good friend to the people, Unlike Coyote, who stole and lied, Poof Poof always told the truth.

If the author made this story up on his own, how did he get Poof Poof's description so close?

George's Big Brother

Actually there may be just a bit more to this story. Because there's still one giant salamander story I haven't told you about yet. Partly because the account was taken further afield and heard second hand. But mostly because it wasn't George, although it might well be his big brother---

Many years ago, in what amounts to a former life, I worked as a firearms engraver. My biggest client was an interesting fellow who owned a monster pawn shop in Redding California. He was a skeptical person, as needs to be, in order to run a pawn shop. Yet he had an open mind and was not afraid of mysteries. Whenever I visited the shop to pick up 'blank' guns, we'd talk and on one such visit, I happened to mention my run in with the 'Poof-Poof."

Hearing this, he became very exited and insisted on telling me about an incident a friend had shared with him, concerning an encounter he'd had while fishing a wide stream in the Trinity River Area, north of Redding.

He'd just flicked his lure into a dark pool, lying under an overhang on the opposite bank, when the line went tight but didn't move. He jerked, but felt no give. Figuring he'd snagged a root, he realized he had no choice but to wade across and

66

unhook the lure, or else he'd loose it.

So he waded across the stream, following the tightened fish line into a shaded pool under an overhang and right up to it's snagging point, the mouth of a 5 foot salamander. He chose to cut the lure, rather then fight over it.

I found this fellows' story especially interesting for 2 reasons. The size, of course--- it was nearly twice that of our local boys. But also that it was encountered underwater, that was a first for me.

Years later, I discovered some articles about underwater monsters by Loren Coleman, eminent Cryptozoologist, while hunting for information on George. Instead, I found a localized history of another race of Giant Salamander sightings, with a range only a short distance east of mine. There were 4 accounts of another Giant salamander sighted in the Trinity Alps that was at least as large if not larger then the one in my friend's story. Accounts from the 1920s described monsters of 5 to 9 feet long--- all living underwater, either in mountain lakes or rivers. Several fishermen attempted to snag them with fish hooks, trying to capture one. One man said he actually got the critter as far as the shore but couldn't move it any further, due to snowy weather.

Check the map, I've put together; doesn't it suggest 2 separate species?

In 1939, a herpetologist, a George S. Myers, was summoned to look over a strange beast, caught by a fisherman, just south of Redding, on the Sacramento River. He identified it as some form of the Asian Giant Salamander. As it was only 2 feet long, it had to be a youngster.

The Asian Giant has 2 subspecies and is found in China, Japan and Mongolia in the same landscape as the Trinity Alps. It lives underwater and tops out at 5 feet. Gray, wrinkly and primitive looking, it has a baby brother that lives in the USA in our southern states. Also completely aquatic, it grows to 2 feet long and is called a Hellbender. The Native Americans used to hunt and eat them. The Asians did the same with their big brothers in China and Japan. In fact, in regards to both of these species, I read that they used to be both larger and more numerous before people thinned them down for dinner.

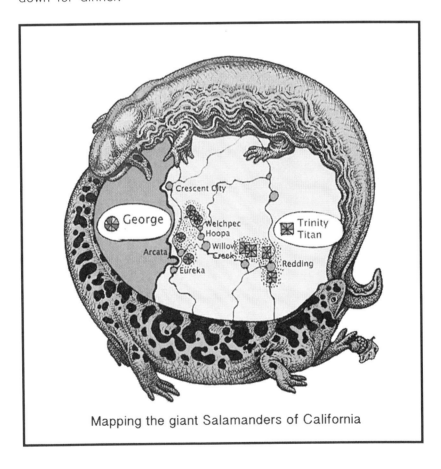

Mapping the giant Salamanders of California

But Myer's monster didn't resemble either of these in it's coloring. Instead of a muddy background sprinkled with black spots, it was dark brown with well defined yellow spots. Coleman suggested it might represent a separate species.

If you check the fossil archives, you'll discover that there was one form of Asian Giant Salamander measuring up to 7 feet if not longer, that lived in this area of North America right up until the Miocene. So it's not inconceivable that they existed here in respectable numbers until recently.

So what changed? When the Gold Miners came into the area, the Native People retreated to higher ground, hidden safely away from the dangerous newcomers. With less available game at that elevation, I wonder if they resorted to hunting the Giant Salamanders, until, by the 1920s, the Monster of the Trinities was barely even a memory?

Except for the odd survivor who swallows your lure.

A Mother Ship comes to the Dance

As I've mentioned, earlier, I discovered many ways to make people talk.

The best was the t shirts we had printed. Passive information beacons---walk this way!

Often, people would snag me if I just sat still long enough.

Once, while waiting to talk to our C.P.A, sitting outside his office, his secretary commented on my UFO Expert t shirt and informed me that her boyfriend had had several sightings, himself. And before I could ask, she assured me that he'd be happy to tell me about them. He found the subject very interesting. She promised to tell him that I'd be calling them that night.

Dan turned out to be a friendly, straight spoken man, who gave the impression of having a curious and open mind. He was a long distance trucker, raised in the Eureka area.

1st Account

At the time of his first encounter, Dan Broad was a young man. The date was May 10th, 1979. He emphatically declared (several times, in fact) that he'd remember that date till the day he died.

His (now ex) wife and he were driving to a dance, which was being held out of town, in a building surrounded by tall conifers. At that time, the region was made up of small towns, scattered among huge expanses of timberland.

Dan pulled into the parking lot. He and his wife had just stepped out of the car, when an object, resembling a giant silver ice cream cone, bobbed up behind the dance hall, appearing directly in front of them, rising just above the tree line.

Nearly paralyzed from fear, they fell against the car, and slid down low enough to feel hidden, while they watched the show.

At first, it seemed to rock back and forth in place. Then it suddenly arched into the sky and dropped again, stopping just above the tree line. Then it repeated the procedure. After several more of these arch and dives, it shot west, over the ocean.

Dan estimated that it measured about 75 yards across. It lowered to about a telephone pole and a half's length from the ground. He thought it was about 500 feet away from them.

The construction was seamless as far as he could tell. No protuberances. He thought there might have been windows on the top part, but wasn't certain.

Outside of a faint humming sound, they heard no noise. He did observe a turbulence in the surrounding trees, when it dipped down, as well as a mirage like heat distortion effect, similar to smoke, that followed in it's wake.

Although the sighting seemed to take 5 minutes, Dan admitted it actually could have been as short as 1 or 2. Time seems to stop at times like this, and he wasn't checking his watch.

Until it left, neither of them could move. Knees having buckled at first glimpse, Dan was leaning against the car for support. After they were sure it had left, they managed to find their legs again and walked across the lot and into the building.

Entering the door, and still obviously in shock, people immediately began to approach them, asking if they'd seen a ghost and such like. Dan remarked that it was like witnessing a train wreck; impressed on his mind as though it had happened yesterday.

2nd Account

His second account happened later the same year, in November. He was trucking, and had almost finished a long run, heading for his home in Eureka.

It was only when he hit the outskirts of town about midnight, that he first noticed a large black triangle craft hovering in the sky above. Although it felt as if he only watched it for a few minutes, when he got home he discovered he'd lost about 3 hours of time. He also had nightmares for some time, following this experience, which was not the case after his first sighting.

A third account he offered, happened not to him, but to a friend, a Crab Fisherman and the captain of his own boat. I was given the fellows phone # but never followed up.

It happened around 1986, when his friend (call him Joe) was out at sea crabbing. A light appeared far ahead of them, barely above the surface of the waves. It grew brighter, apparently heading straight for their boat. Joe quickly realized how huge it was; estimating it to be several football fields across. It actually looked like it intended to collide with their ship.

But, instead, it plunged into the ocean some distance away from them, while still moving forward. As the crew watched in shock, the leviathan sized light passed below their vessel, filling the sea beneath them in every direction.

This was an interesting report, but maybe I'm just jaded? I've heard of others that were similar. Sounded like a UFO went submersible. Hardly mystifying.

But they're not all so pat. Years later I was to hear another Unidentified Submersed Object story that was bizarre even for the genre---

Under the Waves

One of the benefits of gathering strange accounts along the coast is that objects are not only observed in the sky but beneath the waves as well. One of Mr. Broad's accounts described a UFO diving and then moving underwater. Usually they are witnessed a ways from the shore. But not always.

Several years back I set out to visit the area of Bray's Point on the middle Oregon coast, in order to find out first hand the truth about some internet reports regarding mysterious singing metal boxes, submerged in the shore.

Although only mid morning, a number of vehicles were already parked along the muddy dirt turn off at Bray's Point. As I pulled into an empty spot, a youngish man and older woman pulled their car in beside mine.

"Are you here about the boxes?" asked the young man, leaning out the window. We got out to talk. It turned out that John and his Mother lived on the hillside, along the coast, not far away from Brays point. He'd just seen the story online, himself, and had come down to investigate. I told him I was serving as go between for 'real' researchers (as in 'not me') and he wanted to help. So we joined forces, making our way down the beach and querying anyone who appeared approachable. No one had seen a thing, as it turned out, despite the fact that most of them were also there because of the boxes. (Later we found out this 'story' originated from an article published in the Examiner, written by a shady journalist.)

Interestingly we also met a woman from NOAH, who maintained emphatically that if there were any beached metal boxes they were buoys. She'd heard that one had been sighted here and was looking for it. And the singing? Well, you know how sand sounds in the wind when it's sprayed against something metallic? I suspected her story would be the closest to what happened, if anything. Oh well. Worth finding out for myself.

But then, before leaving, I asked John my favorite question and was immediately and richly rewarded. He'd had many strange experiences, but one in particular especially stood out.

It was 2007 and he was strolling with a female friend on the beach at night in the area of South Beach, below Newport, Oregon.

As they walked along the shoreline, they became aware of a deep cobalt colored light hovering 'like a beach ball' at about 4 feet off the ground. It was floating about 150 yards ahead of them and did not seem to be moving.

John thought that someone might be holding it, (like a flashlight?) and he ran toward it, to find out. However, as soon as he got to within 50 feet of it, the light sped directly away from him at the very same speed he was moving at, so he wasn't able to get any closer. When he slowed down, it did the same. He then started to walk backwards, out of curiosity, and the light followed at the same speed. They continued in this way until they had returned to the place John had originally found it. There it stopped.

Reflections of a Crop Circle Case

So he continued back to join his friend who was still in place, waiting for him.

Suddenly his friend asked him what were those lights under the water? He looked at the tide and saw an area of phosphorus, a completely natural phenomenon. In distinct contrast to the 5 lights submerged within it, moving in tandem through the phosphorus along the shoreline at about 55 miles an hour. They looked like car headlights and were set in a straight line. When they reached the point where the blue orb had settled, they veered off to sea, as though circling in an arc, the light being midpoint. John said it was like the light served as some sort of a beacon or marker.

While John and friend were standing there digesting this, another group of lights came into view from the same direction as the first, banking off the blue light like the group before. And then another. In all, they witnessed 5 groups of lights approach and curl away from the beach. They could see the water displacement above them as they came near shore.

When the 5th group of lights reached the blue orb, all the lights went out, including the blue orb. John said that at that moment something else happened that scared him. Everything suddenly went completely silent. No waves crashing, wind whistling, it was like a vacuum. His immediate sensation was that something important had changed and they needed to get away from there, fast. He thought something bad might happen to them, if they remained.

John has worked for a security outfit, is a tall sturdy man, was a kick boxer. He seemed intelligent, curious and confident, much like his mother, who also weighed in during our conversation. He stressed that though he's not a fearful person, he has some sensitivity and could feel an actual physical change in the atmosphere when the lights went out.

Valenya

The Ghost of Mapleston Mine

The Lady was welcome company, being as we were living far from any other neighbors. Once we got used to her, we tended to think of her as a living friend, just one dimension removed.

Before we met, I dreamed of her. We were moving to North Eastern California, having joined forces with Terry's brother Ric (also a jeweler) as partners; planning to open up a jewelry store. Living upstairs in the stock room, while looking for raw land on which to build our own home turned out to be our only option. There seemed to be no properties with structures already in place that were affordable, that weren't too far out into the boonies to be able to commute to work.

The dream started with me sitting in the back of a pickup, enjoying the view. Until the dirt road turned narrow and rocky, winding around a sheer mountainside. Suddenly it opened out into a beautiful hidden valley with a small pond and an old gold mind with the ruins of cabins and more. There was a woman still living there, and I knew she was a ghost.

We'd planned to look at three properties that next morning. There wasn't room for us all in the cab of the

Realtor's truck so I opted to sit in the truck bed. And the very first place we looked at was the valley in my dreams. The goldmine was located on the property adjoining ours, now long abandoned. The whole area had once been thickly packed with mines and miners during the gold rush, but few people remained in the scattering of mobile homes and ancient bungalows, that followed both sides of the river. There was a log cabin still standing on piers on the vacant property directly below us and it felt like it might have belonged to the Lady. We bought the Mapleston place that day, and began building a house on a high meadow at the top of the property on our weekends. Within the year we'd moved in. And that's when the Lady started to visit.

Valenya

At first it was just a feeling. I'd told Terry about my dream, and whenever I felt like she was around, I'd mentioned it. Often, he felt her when I did. Sometimes we'd even talk to her when we both felt she was around.

She had a thing about the clocks. We'd work in the jewelry store Monday through Friday, living upstairs in the stockroom. Friday evening we'd arrive home on the mountain with groceries and I'd wonder if it was time to start dinner? And I'd look for the little battery powered clock that sat on the kitchen counter. Only it wouldn't be there. Sometimes it would take a moment for me to remember. Oh, that's right--- Where could she have put it? This time?

And I'd get down on my hands and knees and peer under the two sofas first; she liked them the best. Not always there, but always on the floor and under furniture. Since it was a small house, essentially one room with a loft, it never took me long to find it.

What was she trying to say? Or was it just her sense of humor? I didn't feel like she was trying to frighten us, it was just her joke.

We realized early on that it couldn't be humans messing with us. Our place was only reachable by taking the aforesaid steep narrow dirt road that took an hour each way driving at 10 miles an hour. To end up at our locked gate, a full mile from our also well locked house. Plus nothing was ever stolen, no tire or shoe tracks, no lock jimmying. Nothing was ever touched. Except that clock. And that, almost always.

I often wondered what we would have seen, had we had a video game camera trained on the clock while we were gone? Did she move it right after we left or just before we returned? Would we have seen a clock start to wobble and fall off the shelf, then drag along the floor? Would it float down? Or just disappear and reappear under the sofa?

More and more, we began to wonder who our visitor was and where she'd actually lived? There was a crumbling cabin, still standing on the property directly beneath ours. I felt it might have been her home. There were daffodil patches growing near it. Men built cabins and planted fruit trees but flowers meant women.

Ter's brother Ric often came out to visit and sometimes stayed overnight. Since our cabin was small, he'd opt to sleep in his truck. Having pre bucket seats, the long front seat made a serviceable bed.

One warm Summer night, he was sleeping in his truck, windows rolled down to keep cool, when something woke him into instant alertness. He sat up and peered out the front window.

Mostly, he was concerned about mountain lions. There was one living up a gully not far up the mountain above our place; we'd found it's bone caches and heard it's screams.

The moon was full and it was easy to see that there were no mountain lions either in front or to the sides of the truck. Ric turned to the rear window.

There was a woman standing there and she was looking in at him. Or so it seemed. Because of the shadow cast by her old fashioned sunbonnet, he couldn't actually see her face.

She was wearing a calico dress which hung down to her shoes. He noticed that it's hem was fluttering in the breeze.

She seemed filmy and nearly monochromatic. In contrast to the flowers she was holding. A sizable bouquet, he thought it might be meant as a gift to us. Unlike the Lady the flowers were so brightly colored, they nearly glowed from within.

And that was the whole show. She didn't move. She just stood there and stared at Ric. Flowers glowing, hem fluttering. And Ric stared back. After a while, he became bored. He didn't feel threatened by her and she wasn't doing anything interesting. So he lay back down and went to sleep.

But the next morning, before I'd even gotten the coffee going, Ric took me aside and asked me if I'd laugh if he were to tell me he'd seen a ghost the night before. So of course I laughed.

Not at him, --- I was just tickled that out of the three of us, she'd finally chosen to show herself to Ric, certainly the biggest skeptic of the bunch.

So we told him about the clocks. And we all debated how we might find out who she could be.

If she had walked up the road to give us the flowers, maybe she had lived in the cabin below. But how to find out?

The land around us held other mysteries. Poking about the goldmine, we discovered a massive stonework, a water channel that ascended the steep mountain along the sheer cliff face. The construction of it was amazing, if not suicidal. Yet it was eight feet wide at the narrowest spot and still strong enough to serve as a virtual road, ascending the sheer side of the mountain. It ended in a narrow, claustrophobic gully, still occupied by a pot bellied stove and the remnants of a tiny cabin, sitting on a tiny flat which had been chopped out of the sidehill. Who would have willingly chosen to live like that, way up there and why?

Along the ancient foot trail that wound about our mountain, and flanking the old abandoned gold mine, we discovered ancient chop marks on the trunks of trees, about eye level. So old that they were nearly lost in ingrowing bark. A small cut above a long vertical one; what did that signify?

About a year later, we met a local forester who synchronistically lived on the other side of the river from us. He'd spent some years researching the history of our area, and was able to give us a few answers. The cabin at the end of the water channel had belonged to an elderly Native woman who was a diehard hermit. The forester had run across the water channel, himself, years ago, and could confirm it as having been built by Chinese labor, in order to wash the gold sands. The tree cuts were what was originally meant by 'blazing' a trail. Literally cutting 'candles' into the trunks of trees at eye level, along the trail so you couldn't get lost. Small chop above a long one; the flame above the candle.

And he knew about our Lady as well, it turned out. Everything but her name, at least.

The flat we lived on had long ago housed a man and wife, though their cabin had rotted away long ago.

The cabin on the bottom flat had been the residence of a bachelor. And the two men loathed each other. Although they practically lived in each others back pockets, neither one would move away, as though that would be taken as an act of capitulation to the other. So for years they lived, side by side, while simmering at each others proximity.

Then the married man died. And his widow promptly moved in with the bachelor in the cabin below. Living with him from then on until till she passed over, herself. It appeared she'd been on much friendlier terms with him then her husband had.

And there her spirit remained? Lingering, until all her neighbors had died or moved away and no one else remained and she was all alone.

But then, just recently, a house had appeared on the flat above hers, and new people had moved into it. Perhaps grateful for our company, she'd picked a bunch of spirit flowers from her garden and floated up the road to visit us.

Our pentagonal house must have puzzled her. Likewise, Ric's Truck parked in the driveway, in front of it.

"What a strange buggy?" she probably thought, peering in. "Where are the horses?" And then Ric popped up! Who was more startled, I wonder?

That winter, we were so often landlocked by snow, that we gave up trying to help Ric run the store. Instead, we tried getting a foothold as jewelers in the California Renaissance

Faire circuit, but without a phone for messages and return calls, it wasn't possible. Way back in the 80s, land lines were all there was and we lived too far out to acquire phone service. Finally we gave up and rented a cabin in the nearby town of Seiad Valley. With a phone and accessibility we found a jewelry slot pretty quick. And so we put our property up for sale. We knew we wouldn't be moving back.

After some months, a young couple, Mike and Trish, bought the place, planning to turn it into a garlic farm. Faire concessionaires, themselves, they made wreaths to sell at harvest style Faires. They didn't mind the remoteness and loved the property. Once they'd settled in, we drove out to visit them and see how things were going.

They were still living in our cabin, but had plans to build a larger one nearby, as well as an airstrip for a small plane (Which they did eventually build).

Right before we left, Trish gave me a funny look and asked me if I knew the house had a ghost?

I realized we'd forgotten to tell them. We'd been living in the town so long that we'd almost forgotten about the Lady, ourselves.

So I asked her how she knew?

"It's the clocks" she replied. "They keep moving around. And we're not doing it---"

So we told them what we knew and compared notes and ideas. They'd also felt her to be female. And that she was friendly, just mischievous; They weren't afraid of her.

But why the clocks?

Valenya

Giant Pot Plantations under Main Street

After we moved back to Weichpec, we often drove back to Goldflats to visit Ric. Catching up on news and gossip at the cafe across the street from the store.

It had been an early run and we were calling it breakfast, when we settled into our chairs.

"You sure picked a funny time to visit." Ric remarked as we sipped our coffees. "The store just got raided last night."

He said it so casually, that it took a moment to sink in. Raided? Does not compute!

Now, robbed, I could imagine. Percentage wise, more Jewelers get murdered during robberies every year then police, even. Every Jewelers fear.

But raided? For what? The stubbed off joint of weed that Ric was usually carrying in his shirt pocket? It wasn't even good pot.

It happened about 4;30 in the afternoon. The store faced North and being a winter day, was already deeply embedded in blue shadow. Already, dark was falling. The last customers had finally left and it was time to put away the day's repair jobs and collect the jewelry in the case displays. Turn the sign in the window to 'Closed,' lock up and head home.

Ric was just finishing up with his last repair when both the doors burst open, at the same time, front and rear. And 6 Swat Agents, dressed in black paramilitary gear stormed into his little jewelry shop, from both ends.

One pushed a rifle against Ric's chest. "Where is it?!?" he demanded. Ric had no answer for that, so he didn't.

Then a dog was brought in and led all about the store; sniffing at everything but stopping at nothing.

Next, a number of the agents started hopping up and down on the floor. They'd hop in place for a few moments, then move over a few steps and start up again. Ric said they made him think of a bunch of weird kangaroos.

At the same time, the guy with the gun kept demanding to know where 'it' was?!? But the way he was pointing it was making Ric too nervous to dare to ask him what it was?

Then Ric noticed that one of the hoppers was jumping dangerously close to the floor stash hidden under a carpet, where Ric had been holding his Mom's treasures (she had no home safe). He broke out of paralysis in order to warn him of this, so he wouldn't break through and smash them.

At this the hopper stopped. So did the others. They all looked somewhat less edgy after all that exercise.

And then they finally told him what 'it' was that they were looking for.

The secret staircase. That led down to the pot plantations in the abandoned gold mining tunnels under Main Street.

Well, of course---THOSE Pot Plantations! You should have said so!

Except for his stress level being as high as it was, Ric would have laughed out loud. OK; where's the hidden cameras? But that gun was still pointed at him.

Ric thought for only a moment, before he figured out

what they were probably looking for.

His shop took up half of the bottom story of a historical 2 story building. Which had been split into 2 shops, set side by side. In fact, there was such an underground staircase in the building, although it wasn't any secret. And it did lead down to an ancient tunnel, built by gold miners, way back in the 1800s. But it was located in the store next door, not in his. And there was a big wide wall separating them. Close, but no cigar. Sorry guys.

So he told them that. At which point they deflated; their bust having gone bust. The gun finally lowered.

Now Ric was curious as to why they'd thought he might have such an ambitious set up going in the first place, let alone in such an unusual spot? To set up such a raid, 6 guys and a dog, they would have had to have been pretty sure they would find something.

It turned out that an imaginative meter reader had been the catalyst. The meter for the whole building, once a single residence, but now divided into 2 shops and several apartments, was still read as one charge, not as separate accounts. And the meter reader had noticed that the water and electric usage had been surging in the last couple of months. He knew there were staircases in some of the shops on that street that led down to the original underground gold mines, that the old town had been built directly on top of.

So he put 2 and 2 together and came up with 5. The electricity was obviously being used for giant underground cannabis gardens! And he hurried off to inform on Ric, whom he had long had a grudge against, anyway.

Hearing that, Ric easily figured out the rest.

And he explained to the agents that the apartments above the shop had recently been rented out to several families of migrant farm workers. It's dirty work; they took a lot of hot showers. And he'd noticed that they invited all their buddies to come up and do the same. In fact, the hot water was running pretty much nonstop nowadays. So much so that he now left buckets on the floor in the workshop, set out to catch the constant drippage coming from his ceiling, leaking from the ancient corroding pipes directly above.

And Ric suggested gently that the next time any thrilling rumors about him or his shop started to surface, they might want to come over and just ask him what was up. He'd be happy to tell them. That way they wouldn't need 6 guys, a dog, and all that artillery.

When I first wrote this chapter, although it seemed essentially mundane it was simply too bizarre to leave out of the book. It wasn't till I ran it past a friend who became incensed by the account of the rough police handling, that I thought to tell him the rest of the story. And he insisted I tag it on as well. He was absolutely right. It changes everything.

The reason I hadn't done it earlier---it 'outs' the identity of the local sheriff's station by proximity. But it's been 20 years and the bust wasn't their idea to begin with. I'm sure they realize I'm not pointing the finger at them.

If you ever drive out Mount Shasta way, you might want to stop and rest at the Veteran's Memorial park and Sculpture Garden, created by none other then the aforsaid Ric deLugo. The product of an inspiration, to create a living memorial in the shadow of Mount Shasta, dedicated to fallen vets. To be composed of sculpture created by artist Dennis Smith and Ric, and conifer forest, one tree planted for every fallen vet. As Ric (himself a Vietnam vet) wryly observed, it was one way to plant a forest no one would ever dare to suggest cutting. And it would be a big forest.

A lofty vision. I was honestly amazed when the forest service actually allowed Ric to make use of their land. Only Ric could have pulled something off like that.

But it needed irrigation. And that gets expensive. Coming out of pocket from a small town jewelers income? Not likely.

Not long after the thrilling non-bust Ric walked down to the Sheriff's office to reemphasize his suggestion that they communicate with him in the future to avoid similar incidents. Sitting in the impoundment yard he noticed a big pile of waterline, seized from real pot operations. And he had an idea.

He knew the officers were probably a little embarrassed about the recent fiasco; it being a small town gossip travels fast and hard. And he knew many of them personally as reasonable folks; he repaired their jewelry and some of them lingered in the store to visit just like his other customers.

So he made a different suggestion then the one he'd initially intended. How would they like to make a donation to the Living memorial in the way of irrigation line? And he got it!

Their backing certainly didn't hurt a bit in gaining him other local support for the project, either. And supplied with water, the little trees grew. When I last visited, it was a true forest.

Lets walk this back. If he hadn't gone to the substation he wouldn't have gotten the line. If he hadn't been 'busted' he wouldn't have gone to the substation, to notice those piles of waterline. Nor would he probably been given the line, even if he'd asked. I smell a set up by the other side.

For Ric, I'm sure it wouldn't be the first one---

Ric is an unusual person to begin with. If he tells you about a strange experience he had, you'd better ramp it up a few degrees past the curve.

Born into a military family, his first memories were of overseas. For example, of hiding in a little tent, while his mother held off invaders with a flare gun, during a riot in Morocco.

After his parents divorced, his mom, Ric and younger brother Terry lived in Riverside California. Bea took a job at a military installation and was only home during the daytime on the weekends. And Ric fell in with the local gangs and started getting in trouble.

Then Bea married again, to Woody, a drill sergeant. Deciding it was his job to straighten out Ric's trajectory he offered him the choice of Youth Authority or Jail.

Ric chose Youth Authority. Being an intelligent kid he was taken under the wing of one of the councilors who taught him woods craft, focused him and simply gave him the sort of adult male attention he needed. John was exactly the person he needed for a mentor.

Historical hiccups---have I mentioned yet that Ric and Terry's natural father was a de Lugo and even supposedly a Count? His prolific and prosperous Spanish family received land grants from Spain in the 1700s in the region of Southern California, at one point encompassing all of present day San Bernardino and most of Los Angeles county. Before they sold out to the gold miners, Mormon immigrants and ranchers, they were essentially the resident royalty in Southern California for nearly 100 years.

During the last phase of their reign, they made their

money from raising cattle, which they sent northward, to supply beef to the miners in the gold fields of the Sacramento area. I would like to identify the family Ric's mentor John belongs too, but his family was not willing. So let me say that the Gold Rush started with Johns forebear, who is prominently featured in the first chapter in California history books as discovering ore at his mill. Even his full name is the same as his ancestor.

His fore bearers and Ric's certainly had business dealings together and probably even knew each other personally as the patriarch Don Antonio was raised in Northern California. That's strange enough. But wait.

When Ric's term in Youth Authority was up he went home and promptly fell in with the same crowd as before. And got into trouble again. Now, being too old for Youth Authority, Woody gave him a new choice. Jail or the military.

And Ric chose the Military.

Before he left for Viet Nam, he had to make a decision. Who to leave his treasures with? He had a few of the last of his families heirlooms, the most important being the family sword. He didn't trust it to Woody or his mom or any of his friends. Then he thought of John and tracked him down. John agreed to hold it for him till he returned.

The military made use of his 'talents' of youth and anger and trained him as an interrogator. By the time Ric was released, he'd realized that he'd probably been encouraged to torture a number of innocent old Papa-sans just on the off chance that they knew anything.

When he returned home only Woody was there. He congratulated Ric on becoming a man. Ric yelled that Woody had only made him a murderer, which didn't go at all well.

Woody grabbed a firearm and chased Ric out of the house. And Bea never even knew he'd come home.

Next Ric went to look for John. But he couldn't find him and was told by neighbors that he'd moved.

There being no reason to stick around, Ric moved, himself. To Ventura, where he eventually started up a shop creating jewelry and selling imports.

Then, Ric moved up to Black Mountain, just south of the Oregon border in Northern Cal and opened up a jewelry store. For a while, we worked with Ric as partners. The years went by. Eventually Ter tracked down his Mom and Woody (still in Riverside) and they reconnected. And then so did Ric.

Next, Bea decided to move up to his town to live nearby (Woody's protests notwithstanding) and once again they were a family.

When we became involved in the Faire circuit and moved back to Weichpec, we'd often come back to visit and catch up. On once such visit, we'd barely got settled in the back room, when Ric mentioned with a funny smile that he had something to show us. And he gestured at a rolled up towel sitting on a bench in the corner.

He explained that he'd been working at the bench recently, when a stranger had walked into the store, a tightly wound towel cradled in his arms. As he set it down on the counter and began to unwrap it, he explained to Ric that he'd been left with a valuable relic to guard many years ago, but had lost contact with it's owner. That morning, having finally given up on his quest to return it, he'd decided to find out what it was worth and perhaps sell it. He'd checked out the addresses of all the jewelry stores in the area. And although Ric's was arguably one of the smallest ones and also located furthest from his home in Etna, he had an impulse to start with it.

As he finished unwrapping the sword. Ric looked up at his face. Although now concealed with a beard and bearing the creases of age, there could be no mistake.

And then John recognized Ric as well.

Now Ric got up and laid the towel on his bench. And unrolled it, revealing to us the family sword of the de Lugos. The family treasure had been returned to the eldest son at last.

What were the odds? Both men had moved from the base of California to it's very uppermost border, setting within an easy hours drive of each other. And why did John decide to visit Ric first? Whatever, John soon became a back room regular, stopping in for coffee whenever he came to town---

Bartley, the Black Ninja Dangler

Sometimes I think the stories I've heard concerning humans alone easily beat out those of UFOs or Bigfoot for high strangeness. Like this one. And I'll bet there's one cowboy out there who would agree with me---

We met Bartley when we first worked in the shop in Goldflats. He was the handyman for the whole building, at least that was his job title. In reality, I wonder how he ever got the job; I can't recall him ever fixing anything.

Not that the building didn't badly need a handyman. Charming and stately but elderly and endemically leaky, everything was decomposing, especially the metal pipes.

Bartley got called to our shop a lot, at first. But nothing he did ever seemed to make any difference. The toilet always leaked, ditto the pipes above our ceiling. We'd hear the shower turn on in the apartments above and run to grab the buckets before the ceiling erupted.

He was a funny little guy. He had a 'banty' personality and strutted when he walked. He drove a huge motorcycle, which he always parked on the sidewalk in front of our shop, neatly blocking our door to all but our narrowest customers. Which the police always immediately noted and ticketed. And which always made him mad. A prickly fellow, but he seemed harmless enough?

Since he never actually fixed anything we got used to doing repairs ourselves and we quit calling him out. So we didn't notice when he wasn't around anymore.

And it wasn't till Ter and I had quit the store and moved back down river that we heard what had happened to Bartley.

It was during a visit to see the family, Ter's brother and their mom, that we heard the news. It was only a couple days ago that Bartley had been cut down from his tree---

Bartley had decided to leave handymanning, to take up freelance moonlighting in the most literal sense. Sneaking around at night as a paid assassin. Or that was the plan. Only he wasn't very good at that job either.

He had actually found a customer, too. His first client was to be a woman who had apparently grown tired of her husband, a cowboy, but was too lazy to divorce him.

Bartley had even had the foresight to draw up and have her sign a contract, stipulating the terms and payment. I wonder who he'd planned to show it to, if she stiffed him?

The hit should have been simple. It would be a night job. The Cowboy and his wife lived alone, in a lonely RV, parked on a remote patch of scrub land scattered with patches of stunted oak. Lots of cover to hide in. No close neighbors.

Still, in order to make himself harder to see in the dark, he donned a black ninja outfit, which he'd acquired for the job.

Bartley parked his car off the long driveway, a good

distance down the driveway from the RV. Then he snuck up to take a look. He needed to make eye contact with his accomplice, so she'd know to move away from her husband. And he especially needed to see where the Mark was sitting.

He hadn't considered the possibility that he might not be able to do either. Even on it's lowest side, the floor level of the RV was a good 4 feet above the ground. The lowest windows were up past his head. Unless he crept up the steps to the deck he couldn't see into them. Way too risky.

So what could he do? Bartley noticed a large scrub oak, standing alongside the RV, it's branches overhanging the roof. He could climb the tree and peek through the living room windows.

So that's what he did. Except he wasn't quiet enough. As he grappled his way up the trunk, the tree began to sway, setting the branches scraping against the sides of the RV.

And the Cowboy heard it. What was that? Finally, he informed his wife that he heard something funny. And that he was going to find out what it was. His wife didn't know what to say to that, so she kept quiet, and sat pat.

Bartley hadn't quite achieved window peekage, when the Cowboy stepped out the door. He saw Bartley before Bartley saw him, and sized things up.

Then he stepped back into the house to grab his lariat, which lay coiled against the hallway wall. And before Bartley could attempt to reverse gears, the Cowboy stepped out onto the front porch. Quickly, he fed out a length of rope and tossed it over Bartley's head, cinching him neatly just under the shoulders. Then he tugged.

In trying to jerk against the tug, Bartley lost his balance and fell over backwards in the opposite direction. Or almost. Bound by the lasso, with his upper arms pinned against his body, he found himself dangling from the branch he'd just been perched on.

The Cowboy tied off the other end of the rope and admired his work. It was probably a difficult toss with all the branches in the way. Then he stepped back into the RV to call the cops.

I wonder if they laughed when they arrived. It must have been a rare sight, a dangling black ninja. I wonder if Bartley tried to pretend to be a peeper or such harmless nut? After all, if he'd managed to toss his weapon into the brush, there would have been no way for the police to prove what he was really up to.

Except for the hit contract, which they discovered in his pocket. Yup, he'd brought it along with him. Apparently still suspicious of his employer, Bartley was making certain he received everything he had coming---

Reflections from a Crop Circle Case

Part 3

House Calls and Conferences

Winding through UFO Congresses, English Crop Circles, Mexican UFO Corridors and personal Encounters deep in the woods.

Confession in the Basement

I met Sarah by accident, as usual. It seemed like every 4 months or so we'd run into each other. Maybe in a medical clinic, maybe grabbing a cheap meal in the cafeteria of a college campus. The funny thing was we didn't even know where each other lived, yet we'd bonded immediately upon meeting. We even looked something like sisters. We were both 17 and it was 1967.

I ran into her this time in downtown Fresno. We decided to walk together so we could visit.

She'd been on her way to the temple to talk to her Rabbi. She needed advice. She looked troubled, even more then usual. So I went along and waited outside his office, listening to the cantor. Then we walked back to the place I was staying at at that time, a multileveled Victorian structure that housed a girls home. Much like Sarah, I'd been feeling depressed and confused for some time, and a councilor had suggested to my folks that I might do better in a structured establishment of this sort.

There were always girls on the first and second story and I shared a bedroom with 2 other roommates. No private space there.

So we went down to the dim, low ceilinged basement to visit. No one ever came down here; the light was too bad and it felt claustrophobic. I had an Indian bedspread that I'd been intending to sew up for a caftan and there was a sewing machine down there.

Instead, we were sitting on the floor, on a gray stained wall to wall carpet. I'd given up on sewing; too hard to see. Instead I was listening to Sarah reveal what had been bothering her so much. It was the Fairies.

They were horrible. They visited her. In her room.

"Fairies are real!" she insisted." And they're not cute at all. They're scary! And they're bigger then people say they are, too!" She grimaced, tensing at the memory.

The way she was speaking was making me very uncomfortable. I was afraid she'd need me to tell her I believed her. Because I didn't, of course. Obviously what she was talking about was crazy.

But part of the dread I was feeling also seemed to have something to do with the low ceilings, dim light, and the stark gray surroundings. I didn't understand it then, but now I'm wondering if it might have been those same factors that unconsciously inspired my own dread that compelled her to tell me what she just had.

I don't remember what led up to her confession. And I have no memory of what else she said, describing her fairies. I didn't want to hear it, so I blocked it out. I remember that I just wanted to get away from her.

So, I found an excuse to give up on the sewing and cut short the visit. It was my turn to clean out the kitchen and refrigerator, I explained. Alone. I needed to get to work. And she left.

Now I feel ashamed of my response; the way I pushed her away. But at the time it felt like necessary self protection. Run away! From her or them?

I wonder what else she told me about her fairies? Were they green, blue or just possibly gray? How big were they, exactly? And why were they scary; What did they do? I really wish I'd listened or asked.

About a year later, I ran into her in the local junior college cafeteria. She was sitting alone at a table in a corner of the courtyard, drawing pictures of cartoon birds being strangled by bodiless hands.

She was seeing a psychologist for depression. She understood that she was the bird. It was her own breath, her own voice that was being cut off. But what about the hands? Whose were they? I didn't ask and she didn't offer.

She invited me to visit her, at her house. Instead, I remember turning brusque and disappearing as soon as I could.

I never saw her again.

She was a smart girl. A sensitive person with a good sense of humor. But she still scared me.

Back in 67, who had heard about abductions? There was no framework. If you were a youngster and shiny little beings with big eyes suddenly appeared in your room, to drag you away what would you call them? And what would people call you?

Whenever I hear pronouncements that experiencers must be a bunch of nut cases I have to smile. If so, now why might that be? Maybe not for the reasons a person might think?

Suppose you weren't nuts when the visits began, might your sense of reality not start to wobble seriously after just a few encounters? First by knowing there were frightening things happening to you, that you didn't understand, much less dare to talk about. Or else normal 'sane' people would tell you to shut up, lock you up or just avoid you. But in some way, you would certainly be punished for being honest. Count on it.

How many friends have I lost over the years, myself, who made some some insulting comment about "those idiots on Oprah who believe they've been abducted" and I felt the need to swing wide the closet doors and educate them?

And how would you not go nuts, if you felt that in order to be acceptable to people you cared about, or who held power over you, you must pretend to deny what you knew was happening to you? It would split you in two.

Sure that could send you around the bend. Not the ETs, themselves, necessarily. But the reactions from other humans.

What really impresses me, in contrast, is how many Experiencers have managed to remain sane.

I appreciate that I wasn't awakened to my own involvement until later in life. I'd already been studying the subject for about 10 years. I had some framework to use in understanding. It wasn't till the mid 90s before I started to remember my experiences, both ongoing and earlier. By then, literature on the abduction phenomena had been out for a good ten years.

Sarah had no such context to draw from back in '67. And no protective buffering memory wipe, either, apparently. Not only was she seeing fairies-which everyone knew weren't real, but the ones she saw didn't even look like fairies should. They were scary and they kept returning.

I hope she finally got a handle on what was actually happening to her. I imagine she probably knows by now---

I still wish I could apologize, though.

The Swinging Party

It wasn't that Martha Wilder was avoiding her room in order to get out of doing her homework. She consistently held an A average and enjoyed school. But it was only when she was sitting alone in her room studying, that she'd hear them, the people on the swing.

At first only a faint murmur far in the distance, it would swell into a full chorus of voices. All speaking at the same time and peaking in volume as they 'swung' right above and over her head. Then dimming down to a murmur again, as they swung away. Then returning, their voices growing loud and articulate once more, swinging past, becoming soft and indistinct. Back and forth, louder and softer. It was scary.

It didn't always happen. But when it did, Martha did the one thing that always made it stop. She got up and went into the kitchen, where her mom was working. And stood next to her in the bright overhead light.

It didn't seem to happen in other rooms. Just her bedroom.

She thought about it a lot. Sometimes, she drew pictures of what she imagined the people looked like, perched on their giant swing.

Martha is my mother and her story is one I've heard many times; sort of a family puzzle. As a child, even before

104

I'd heard her tell it, I usually slept in her childhood room when visiting my Grandparents and I always felt uncomfortable there. I felt like I was not alone. Was her room haunted? And if so, by a whole party of spirits? Why couldn't she see them? And why wouldn't they stop swinging?

John's China Reeds

Have you ever found a pile of change somewhere unexpected, perhaps neatly stacked on a sidewalk, during your morning stroll? Did you wonder if someone had lost it, or whether it had been planted on purpose to see what people passing by might do? What would you think if this happened to you frequently? It happened to me a lot when I was young.

I found money walking, generally. I usually found it in small coinage, sometimes stacked, mostly on the side of the road or sidewalk. Just consistently enough to notice and wonder about.

Once, when I was 10 years old, I was walking down a line of railroad tracks, that divided a huge open field out on the edge of town. As I hopped cross ties, I was absently wishing I had 15 cents. That exact amount plus what I'd already saved would buy me an hours worth of horseback riding in the rental section of the local stables, two blocks away. I lived for these rides and usually had enough saved up over a week to cover an hour on Saturday morning. But not this week; I was just 15 cents short.

Less then 100 feet in front of the spot where I first started wishing, I discovered 3 nickels in a neat stack, placed on a cross tie, mid track. Right where I'd have to see them. I

106

looked in both directions. I was all alone. The wide fields were covered in sparse grass and low brush, no place for a person to hide. And I hadn't even been muttering out loud, just thinking. 15 cents. Exactly the amount I needed.

Forward the video about 8 years. I'm hitchhiking around Europe with my now ex husband, Dan. We did OK traveling up till France, when our rides became extremely infrequent. In reality, we probably spent more of our time walking between towns then riding.

We'd brought along several thousand dollars in travelers checks. Which would have been clever if we hadn't bought such an obscure brand. Cooperative banks turned out to be few and far between and we always underestimated how much money to change when we discovered one.

Often as we'd plod down some seemingly unending highway, my husband would remark that unless I found some money pretty soon, we wouldn't eat tonight. And I'd begin scanning the road ahead.

Usually, I'd find money fairly soon, along the side of the road. Usually spread far apart, scattered like bread crumbs along the shoulder. Only cash, never bills. And yet, always enough to make the difference; even if it was just enough to cover a dry sausage and a loaf of bread. Yet twice it was enough to pay for a meal in a cafe, and once even covered a night in a hotel room. That was certainly a welcome change from our tent. I doubt the French make so much money they feel a need to throw it out of their cars?

I always found lots of that useless aluminum wartime coinage for some reason. If you ever want to watch a French grocery clerk wrinkle up his lip, make like an ignorant tourist and offer him a handful of this stuff.

Later, I was to meet the man I would share my life with. To find out that an old man he'd once lived with, had found not only coins but gold and gold mines. And bodies.

When Terry was about 17 he left home, but being broke and jobless could not find any other place to live. John lived near Terry's girlfriend; on small acreage that he owned. An eccentric but tolerant old gold miner, he invited Terry to move into one of his outbuildings and live there rent free. After chasing out the chickens, Terry did just that.

John wasn't a greedy man, he only mined enough gold to cover his needs. He subsisted off day old bread (half price at the bakery!) and the avocados that grew on the 2 acres of his land located near L.A., on the eastern foothills of San Bernardino. He lived in a stone house which he'd built himself by hand. And looked for gold by dousing a map with a China Reed.

John was a wrestler in his youth and a gnostic leaning Christian. He didn't preach, you had to draw his convictions out of him. He used to mine hard rock for gold in Nevada until repeated and unwarned exposure to covert nearby nuclear testing left him with a terminal case of cancer.

Hard rock mining takes several healthy men. So he moved to the San Bernardino area and doused a map for gold instead.

First he would unroll a map over the kitchen table. He had registered claims in several areas of Southern California and maps for each one.

Then he'd take his dousing tool, which he called a China reed. It was made of 2 long slim sticks, tied together with a bit of either leather or string, which also held a nugget of gold. And he'd douse the map with this.

Then he'd leave his home for a few days to go get his

gold. Since he'd become sicker he did this less and less.

The Government was well aware of his abilities. Occasionally they they would send someone to his house to try to convince him that it was his patriotic duty to tell them where to look for gold.

Maybe his cancer had dampened his sense of patriotic duty. But after being used by his government as an unwitting and now terminating nuclear test subject he felt no urgent responsibility to comply.

As the car rolled up his drive, he'd remark laconically to Terry, if he happened to be visiting, "Here comes Uncle Sap. Wants me to tell them where the gold is buried." And then he wouldn't.

But sometimes it would be a police car rolling up the drive. When John saw that coming, he would pick up his china reeds and hunt down his maps. Getting ready.

And Ter would head home to his chicken coop. It was just too creepy for him.

John would douse the maps for the person the police were seeking. Whether kidnapped or lost, he could find them. He could also tell if them if the person was still alive.

Unfortunately, by the time they'd resorted to him, it was usually a body they were seeking.

The first time he'd done this, was to locate one of his own relatives. No one else could find the body so he'd volunteered to try. After that, he just helped whenever the police asked him to. He felt that his ability to douse for people should be freely offered to any who asked.

Gold was something different.

A Tale of 2 Batteries

2 people needed exactly the same thing. And it was provided as if by providence, but why in such different packages?

My nephew Evan has also experienced several instances of finding money when he really needed it. During his college years, he often found himself running short, but hated to importune his folks. One time when he was nearly at that point, and needed money for food, he found cash in a crumpled brown paper sack waiting just outside of the doors of a grocery store.

A few years ago, he found himself in a very difficult situation. He and some buddies had just spent a frozen night in a motel in Lake Tahoe, during one of the coldest nights ever recorded for that town, a record of minus 15 degrees.

When they awoke in the morning, they discovered a thin layer of snow blanketing the ground and their car battery completely dead, a victim of old age and frozen temps. And they were broke. At least too broke to buy a battery.

Their car was parked at the very end of the motel lot, off by itself, and a good distance from the other cars, which is important to take into account. There was no reason for anyone to have walked by it earlier.

Here Evan continues his story.

110

"Right after trying to start the car for a few minutes, we popped the hood and looked in. I was standing just in front of the driver door, looking under the hood. And right when I said, "Damnit, this is going to be a hundred bucks!", I looked down at my feet, sort of as an admission of defeat. And a hundred dollar bill was lying in the snow exactly where my last footprint had been. If I hadn't gotten out and pushed the snow with my foot by accident, it wouldn't have been possible to see it.

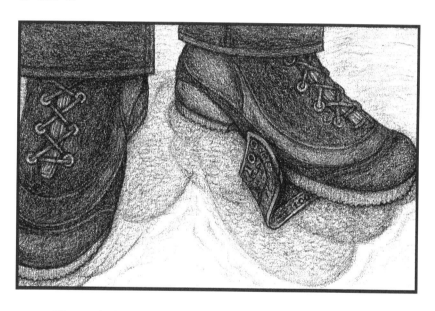

We ended up walking 2 miles across South Lake Tahoe with the dead battery, because we had to exchange it in order to get the new one. After exchanging the old battery, the new one came to $99.96. It couldn't have been any closer to $100."

I couldn't help comparing Evan's find to my find of those 3 nickels when I was a kid. Funny that whoever was providing the money left exactly enough to cover the gap but no more?

While Evan was telling us this story at our kitchen table, Terry was showing great interest. He'd had an experience that was nearly identical, as it turned out. But not exactly---

Terry was also a young man at the time of his story, traveling with buddies and broke. They were heading to Arizona from Southern California. After eating at a truck stop, right on the state line, they returned to their car to find that turning the key got zero response. No mystery there, the battery was dead. He'd had no money to replace it, so he hadn't. And now they were really stuck.

For no really good reason, they decided to look about the shoulder of the road. For what, a free battery store? But almost immediately Terry noticed a battery hidden under a bush. Who would toss away a good battery? he thought, doubtfully. But it wasn't like they had any choice but to check. There was a piece of wire lying nearby so they tested it for spark. Charged and ready! And down the road they went!

It wasn't as fully charged as if it had been brand new, but perfectly adequate for their needs, Ter noted, which I found especially interesting. Maybe the angels are on a budget these days? Besides gracing Evan with just enough money for what he needed, they also gave Terry a battery that was just good enough to wiggle his buddies out of a jam.

The Year of 'You Too'?!

"What did you do for Christmas?"

"Oh, same old. Exchanged rocks, then we talked about Aliens."

Call it a family joke or a family tradition. Really it's both. Crystals are always favorite gifts. And It seems like it's always during the holidays that we exchange the strangest stories.

Sometimes, they're even 'cross exchanged'---

This account belongs to 2 people, in overlap. Mine and my brother's.

Our family had just moved to a new home. And it felt as funny to my brother Will as it did to me, we just didn't talk about it till many years later. Off settling, off kilter. Maybe not bad but certainly not good.

It was a nice property and cheap. It had an inset swimming pool and a big ranch house, a garage, and a workshop repurposed from the original kitchen. It was also covered with dead foliage from being on the market such a very long time. Years in fact. Maybe because it was only one narrow street away from a very active railroad track? Which had us all feeling unsettled for a while, especially when the trains blew their whistles. Probably, that was why I didn't notice the dread at first.

But something really bothered me and I soon started investigating every room in the house, in order to find out where it felt the worse. I peeked over high shelves and cabinets, and pulled out drawers. I found a paperback copy of Star Man's Son on the top shelf of a closet. Which I immediately started to read.

A strange thing began to happen just before I'd drift off to sleep at night. A string of disjointed telephone conversations would fill in my head. Like radio stations skipping and fading. I could hear the conversations clearly. They were totally boring.

"How's your Mom's eczema?" "But her paws were so muddy!" "And you won't believe what they were asking for red onions." to give you an example. All in different voices, bleeding in and out. Hard to sleep with all that noise.

And I soon found the epicenter of the icky feeling. The guest bedroom at the end of the bedroom corridor, which adjoined the living room and craft room. It's windows faced the street. There was a closet and a small bathroom attached on one side. They felt the very worst. The closet had a mirror, and so did the bathroom. I couldn't look in either of them. I didn't like to even be near that side of the room.

And yet, perversely enough, during my first semester of college, I moved into it by choice. It makes no sense. But I felt drawn to it. Almost immediately I fell into an unexplainable daily routine.

My classes were early, ending at noon. Take the bus home, eat lunch, then lie on the bed and take a nap. And fall into my nightmare. Because it was always the same one.

As soon as I fell out, I'd wake up in the dream. Still lying on my bed, in the same room. But I'd sense that something had arrived; something that was frightening me to the point of paralysis. It knew how terrified I was and was gloating over it.

Somehow it was always night in my nightmare, though

it was early afternoon in reality. So it was too dark to see anything. Sometimes I'd scramble off the bed and crawl along the floor, searching for the wall, so I could flip on the wall light switch.

There! ---It worked! The light came on! Nobody in my room. Maybe I was really awake?

But then, all by itself, the light would go out again. The fear would return. And I could feel it playing with me. Finally the panic itself would awaken me.

After nearly two weeks of this program, I had a different dream. This time it was light outside when my Day-Mare began. I got off the bed, feeling drawn to the window. Across the road stood a little girl. Staring at me like she hated me. Before I could wonder about it, without moving, she was suddenly standing right on the other side of my window, only inches away from my face. You could feel her anger towards me. What for? Her face looked dead, puffy and white. Then the lights went out.

Again, it was returning, the invisible dreaded presence, exulting in my fear.

I wish I could remember what happened next. Or at least understand what finally worked. I remember throwing out desperate energy, willing myself to wake up. Because I knew it had to be a dream. Then I felt the presence of someone else, someone new, it felt like a friend?

Now, my dread was receding, the loathsome being was fading. But I wasn't quite awake. As I rose back to consciousness, I heard one line of a song sung three times. "It's your dream, if you know what I mean." it repeated, in a style evocative of Morrison and the Doors.

The same day, I moved back to my old room. Never

had the dream again.

Twenty years later, I was reminiscing with my brother about that house. It was during a family Thanksgiving at Mom's and we were sharing stories and family memories. I told him about my falling asleep phone conversations. "You too?!" He exclaimed, astonished. The same thing had been happening to him, as I, and at the same time, just more mumbly and less comprehensible.

He was also intrigued that the guest room had bothered me too, and asked me what area was the worst. "You too!?" he exclaimed once again, when I told him. "Yeah, I couldn't look in those mirrors either or even use that bathroom."

"Especially at night." he added "I think something really bad happened in there."

I was also surprised to find out that way back during the period when I'd felt compelled to inspect all the rooms in our house, he'd been doing the same. Only he was much more thorough then I.

And he'd discovered that the closet of the 'bad room' had access doors to both the attic and an under house area, which was not exactly a basement, but not open, either. He inspected both, found nothing, but then again, he really didn't know what he was looking for---

My OOBE, a Set up?

Oddly, it was in the very same house that contained the icky haunted room that I also had the most spiritually uplifting experience of my life. And the most surprising.

It began with a small tragedy. My cat, a sweet old calico I'd had nearly my whole life was hit by a car.

I was about eleven years old. We'd just moved several times in the last year, and the kids in each neighborhood were a bit rougher then those in the one before. A shy child, I hadn't made any friends yet. Uprooted and lonely, Purrit had been my only comfort and connection to my past life. She'd slept with me, loved to snuggle and purred loudly. But then she went missing.

When I discovered her car struck, crushed body two blocks away, lying on the side of the road, I fell into a deep depression. My Mom let me adopt a kitten, thinking this might help. I chose without considering very deeply and took the first I saw. Picking a siamese kitten, that had been born and raised in a barn. I should have wondered why it had to be shown to me in a cage.

At home I let her out into the back room we used for crafts. It had piles of boxes of unpacked belongings to provide cover for Jennifer to hide behind. And that's exactly what she did. Whenever I came in to try to visit her, she'd yowl in a heartbreaking terrified way. And scuttle desperately from box to box, trying to escape me. We put down food for her, but she'd always wait till we'd gone, before she'd come out to eat. As wild as as any weasel or badger. And she stayed wild.

I felt awful whenever I thought about her, alone and frightened, hiding behind the fortress of boxes. Probably waiting for us to eat her.

But I also felt helpless to fix things. I finally realized what a bad mistake I'd made in picking her and felt awful about that too. And I missed Purrit so very, very much.

One Saturday, about middle afternoon, following one more unsuccessful attempted visit, I lay on my bed, crying silently. I thought about Purrit laying next to me, how her long fluffy fur would tickle my face. And about her warm rumbling purr. Then I thought of her body, now lying cold and stiff in her 'grave' in our flower bed and really started to sob. I couldn't stop.

After maybe a half hour I wore out, feeling numb and emptied of feeling. Staring upward at the ceiling in a spacey stupor, I felt dead. It was actually a relief.

Then I started to rise up into a sit. I wasn't trying to, it actually felt as though someone had hooked their hands under my armpits and was lifting me up. Actually, it wasn't 'me' that was rising, my body was still lying down. But someone I couldn't see had pulled the other me into a sitting position.

Then, without warning, I was pushed through the wall and into the hallway, which ran from the 3 bedrooms, to face the door of the scary room, which also had a door connecting to the craft room where Jennifer hid.

I barely felt the wall, as I passed through it. There was only some light pressure and then I'd popped through to the other side. But what was I doing in the hall??

I floated just above the floor, bobbing lightly. It felt as

though I was expecting something. I felt a mental tug from the direction of the scary room and turned my gaze that way.

The door was open. And Jennifer was walking through it. Had someone opened the craft room door and let her out? She was heading down the hallway in a deliberate manner and I suddenly 'knew' she was coming to my room. Even though she'd never been there before. I could feel her

119

intention.

Maybe it was the surprise connected to that realization that instantly snapped me back through the wall and right back into my body. Lying on the bed on my back, I sat up and glanced at the opened bedroom door. And Jennifer walked through.

Without hesitation, she hopped on my bed. Moving slowly and carefully, I found a ribbon and managed to tease her into playing with it. Then she fell asleep on the covers. For some reason, she'd suddenly decided to trust me.

Things seemed to improve after that. My depression lifted. And Jennifer soon acted like she'd always been our house cat.

I've often wondered about that experience. It seemed like such a choreographed set up? Someone must have known it was just what I needed. But who it was it that pushed me through that wall and was there only one being involved?

Who lured the kitten out of her safe room, and directed her to mine? And gave her confidence that I wouldn't harm her? And who made someone in the family forget to close the door to the craft room---or did it open by itself?

A Crop Circle Case at the Conference

Sometimes you can go to a UFO Conference and pick up nearly as much by having a concessions table as by attending the presentations. Back when the International UFO Congress was still held in Mesquite Nevada, I had one of those shows.

I remember that Colin Andrews was the keynote speaker, that year and kicked things off with an inspired presentation, despite suffering from a grim case of the seasonal Winter crud. Carlos and Margarite Diaz took the stage together, to talk about the craft currently being seen in their home town of Tepoztlan, Mexico and showed the latest photos Carlos had taken of them. I'd met these folks the year before in Tepoztlan, and really liked them both. I'd witnessed my first UFOs down there, as well, so I wasn't going to miss their talk.

But for me, most of the best presentations took place right in front of our sales table, given by people I didn't even know.

I acted as doorman to one such account. Our table was closest to the door, so I opened it a lot.

The 3rd morning was pretty slow. Ter had opted to go back to the motel room and watch movies on TV.

I didn't mind the slow times, it just meant that people

121

lingered longer and when they did, they told me things.

But by 11 am, the concessions room was pretty much deserted. I was sitting alone at the table, when I spied a tall older fellow on crutches outside the heavy glass doors and heading my way.

I jumped up and pulled open one of the doors and he swung inside. Probably out of courtesy, he visited my table first. All the informational EB Ts and Crop Circle jewelry probably suggested to him that I might be interested in hearing about his experience. He was obviously itching to tell somebody.

From the way he asked me if there were any 'Experts' I could direct him to that collected 1st hand experiences, I realized he'd mistaken the concessions room for the main event, one building down. But his desire to share his story might be too general a plan, all the Speakers had specific areas of expertise. Which I knew, from endlessly rereading the conference lineup. Perhaps if he was to tell me what it was he wanted to share, I could direct him to the most appropriate experts?

Hearing that, he relaxed. I pulled out my conference brochure and went over the speakers with him, quickly realizing he didn't know the first thing about UFOs.

As it turned out, he'd never even meant to stop at the conference at all. He was an independent long distance truck driver and was carrying a load through Nevada. But about twenty minutes ago, he'd seen a billboard, "Welcome, UFO Congress; Mesquite Nevada!" and on impulse turned in at the conference parking lot. His load wouldn't spoil and he was curious. But before he left, he wanted to talk to someone who could tell him something regarding an experience that had happened to him long ago, back when he was a kid in military service.

I think he told me first in order to get up his nerve.

It happened, when he was stationed in the Southwest. A group of soldiers were collected to board a bus and he was one of those selected. No explanations, no questions allowed. No destination was revealed. The windows were covered, so they had no idea where they were going. Not only were they warned not to ask any questions but they were advised not to even think about it later, as "It won't make any sense to you anyway."

The bus stopped somewhere out in the desert. Their job was to pick up what looked like shredded tinfoil from a wide area of land. They were not allowed to talk as they did so.

He agreed that they were right--- it didn't make any sense to him at all. The material he was collecting, the whole situation, the secrecy. Then they boarded their windowless bus and drove back. So once they'd returned he didn't think about it again---for years.

He didn't know anything about UFOs, hadn't even heard of Roswell. But then, recently, he'd seen a show about Roswell on TV. And the old memories surfaced. Interestingly, he was certain the day he collected material was not anywhere near the time of the Roswell crash. Meaning there was more then one?

My interest in his story gave him confidence. He briefly visited the other sales tables, then headed out the door to the conference area, probably to hunt down one of the 'experts' I'd suggested.

He'd barely left the table when a suspiciously normal looking, older middle class sort of fellow walked in the doors. He wandered about for a bit, talking to all the vendors at every sales table, before finally washing up on mine. As it turned out, he was also seeking information, only not for himself. It was for his daughter; he was worried about her.

She was being abducted. Fairly frequently, it seemed.

Also, her 3rd child was very different from the first 2 (not worse, he emphasized) and she had told him that her son was a hybrid.

She couldn't tell her husband. She couldn't bring up ETs or aliens with him. He wouldn't listen, the subject scared him. So she talked to her dad instead.

I was touched at the way this guy was trying to help his daughter. Although he didn't know anything about UFOs, and the subject scared him as well, he believed her and wanted to help.

I suggested a researcher he should talk to, but he was nervous. About being thought a nut, about bothering the 'Expert'. I urged him onward, "Believe me, he will want to hear you!" He promised he would. And headed out the door. On to the Conference building!

It was getting close to to dinner time. Soon Ter would come down and we could throw a towel over the table and sneak away to the buffet. But there was one more person approaching the table.

A young man, early 20s. Casual, intelligent looking person. After a bit of talk, he let me know that he was an experiencer.

"I used to think I was an abductee". He admitted. "Now I realize I'm a hybrid."

Lately, memories had begun to surface, shifting his perspective. Things he'd never understood before were making more sense. The nightmare attacks were looking more like medical check ups and conceptual study courses.

He'd always had an interest in UFOs. Now he'd morphed into an investigator.

When I asked what he did for a living, he said he was a pilot. He'd always loved planes and flying, even as a kid.

First, he flew crop dusters. Nowadays, he was working as a tour pilot, flying tourists over UFO historical sites and hot spots. Sounded like the perfect job for such a person. He gave me his card.

I couldn't help compare him against my Cowbird Chick profile. Tall, more then usually good looking, self motivated, obviously intelligent and he even regarded himself as a hybrid. 20 some years ago, this was still pretty new. The road from identifying as an abductee to an experiencer to a hybrid is an inner journey, invisible from the outside, but it changes one's perspective as you travel along it.

He inferred that he believed he'd found out this last part because they'd let him know. The memories had broken exactly when they were supposed to, as programmed.

This was a theme I would hear again, more and more frequently. All good things in all good time?

Shortly after he left, Ter came down. We covered up the table, and headed off to the buffet.

4 Encounters and an Interview.
A Circular Pilgrimage

Encounter # 1 and 2

Although these happened a year apart, they were virtually a matched set. You'll see what I mean.

I was alone both times, which I'm sure was factored in, if not encouraged in some way. Both times, I'd been feeling tired and crabby and begged off 'doing' that Faire weekend to catch up on stock instead. So Ter was down state, onsite and I was at home.

These days, I'd recognize the 'I need to be alone or I'll burst' feeling as a sign of impending contact. Emotional button pushing to cut you from the herd.

I'll start in the order I remember things. Actually, it was a circular experience, and order was somewhat subjective.

#1

It happened on Saturday night, I think, in September of 1995. I'd worked at the bench until eight that night and then tagged stock until 10. Then I went to bed, downstairs and fell right out.

And abruptly awoke, several hours later, to a stinging on my skin, mid spine, and what sounded like the world's largest road grader, grinding, scraping away, right above my cabin. Actually it sounded like some other sort of machine than a vehicle. But what could it be?

It was a 2 part sound--- alternating between a rasping scraping noise and a popping sound, like a stick drawn over rails on a fence. The 2 sounds seemed to be connected, slightly overlapping, like breathing out and breathing in.

But it was loud! It seemed like it might be moving east to west, and was now passing over the house.

I jumped out of bed to check the time; Twelve o'clock exactly. Then I started opening windows, so I could hear it better. Still, I couldn't get a bearing on what it could be. I couldn't remember where the tape recorder was, then I realized the batteries would be dead, anyway anyway. Couldn't think of anything more clever to do to get evidence, so I just stacked a pile of magazines on my desk and set the clock on the top of it pointing backwards. I wanted to be able to prove to myself in the morning that this hadn't all been a dream. I had to have been awake in order to have done this.

The huge machine still seemed to be grinding westward. Moving away from me, it sounded to be maybe a quarter mile away and fading. Now I could barely hear it. In frustration, I wished that it would return, so I could commit it's sound to memory.

And then it did. Or else it suddenly grew louder. Either way, it worked. And so fast that I was somewhat suspicious that someone must had overheard my mental request.

Then it 'turned (?)' and either resumed it's path West or grew quieter, hard to say which. Soon it was gone.

I found a pencil and paper and wrote down everything that had happened, from the moment I awoke, the time, the sound I'd heard. I put the note on top of the magazine pile and the clock on top of the note.

At this point, I started to tone down and relax. And I

also became aware, once more, of the raw spot on my back. It felt as if I'd been stung. Or skinned.

I reached around to feel the area. Right over my spine, mid thorax, was a small depression, painful to the touch. Maneuvering a flashlight and a mirror, I could make out that it was circular and shallow, maybe a quarter of an inch in diameter. Like a water blister with the skin pulled off. It felt fresh. It wasn't a spider bite, and I couldn't somehow have done it myself. In fact, it was possibly on the only area of my back that I could barely reach even to touch.

I thought about that uneasily when I finally went back to bed. I read for a long time before I could fall asleep again. But eventually I did.

Then I woke up the next morning and got my second surprise.

#2

The moment that I awoke, I remembered everything that had happened the night before. As well as what had happened the year before, and on the same night exactly. And I hadn't even known about that visit till just then.

It wasn't the same experience, very different, in fact. And shorter as well, at least the part I recall. But I knew they were connected.

Like the night before, one year ago, at exactly this point in the Faire, I'd also elected to stay home and work. Unlike last night, however, I hadn't been able to sleep, so I'd sat up reading till nearly midnight. Finally I laid down, but I still couldn't sleep.

Our cabin sat at the end of a long dirt road, nestled in tall fir trees, set on top of a mountain. No light pollution; you could see our neighbors across the river valley only as tiny lights. And no headlights reaching us from the road, a mile below. I could easily make out the constellations through the high windows, to the south of my bed.

At first I couldn't tell if it was my eyes. Then the rhythmic pulses of light I was registering outside the windows grew brighter. What was doing it? Who was doing it? Why was it pulsing? And so absolutely silent?

I didn't like this at all, it was making me confused and anxious. I remembered pulling the quilts over my head, so I wouldn't have to see. I don't want this to be happening now, I thought, miserably. While I waited. When I woke up the next morning I'd forgotten.

Then it was a whole year later and I was suddenly and completely remembering. But how could I have forgotten anything like that? And how much of the timing of the recall was programed at the time of forgetting?

Of course that brought up so many possibilities; were there still other previous visits still unremembered, tightly locked away? How many others?

Several days after visit #1 had occurred, Terry came home. I showed him the skin punch and told him the story behind it. Asked him what he thought. He was baffled as to what could have made it. I got the same reaction from my Mom.

Then things began to happen. A series of connected synchronicitys that sent my steps in motion, seemingly directing the whole show, and eventually dropping me into the Crop Circle of my dreams. The connections were interesting, if not suspicious.

Roll back the tape to 1990 when my brother gave me a

copy of Circular Evidence as a birthday gift/challenge. Explain this! A friendly disagreement we'd maintained for some years was whether or not UFOs were real.

His opinion was yes. He'd been reading about them since Junior High. My opinion was no. I hadn't read about them at all or I wouldn't have deemed myself such an expert.

Whether they were tied with UFOs or not, crop circles were a genuine mystery and I couldn't argue with him about that. With Colin Andrews breaking trail for the rest of us---at that point in time it was basically just him and partner Pat Delgado in the field full time,---we had somewhere to begin, regarding Crop Circles. And it looked like they kept tying in with both UFOs and synchronicitys, although it seemed like they shouldn't.

For myself, the spiral path completed it's first circle when I took part in the Mexico run. And heard the Road Grader sound on the Crop Circle tape. Then witnessed the 2 doughnut craft on the following night.

It started with borrowing the wrong video from my Mom. The cover box described a video on Roger Leir and implants, but the DVD actually inside was about Stephen Greer and his C.C.E.T.I. trip to Mexico. I hadn't checked before I'd grabbed it. I couldn't bring it back to swap for the one I'd actually wanted; my Mom lived too far away. So I watched it and was amazed at all the activity. I remember jumping up and announcing to Terry that I had to get down there and see for myself. I couldn't though, there was no money, and I knew it.

Not 2 months later, I was invited to take part in a UFO research run spearheaded by Colin and Synthia Andrews. Destination, Mexico, covering the same areas, talking to the same people as Greer's group had previously.

That night, I dreamed of packing a suitcase, while a refrain repeated in the background, chanting like a musical chorus. "Straight circle, divide! straight circle, divide!"---. When I woke I wondered, what's a straight circle? It sounded like a contradiction. Not long after that I signed on to the team. And then as happens so often, once I'd I'd committed to it, I found the money. Just enough.

Not two months later, I found myself sitting with a group of researchers and other group members on a rooftop in Mexico, playing a tape recorder, attempting to get the attention of any friendly craft passing overhead. First we played recordings taken from UFO sightings. I was really hoping I'd hear 'my' sound, but no such luck. Then we flipped over the tape. It read Crop Circle Sounds. First it played the so called Grasshopper warbler sound, picked up in the field. It obviously wasn't that of a bird. Odd sound. Then it was played slower and something tickled my brain. Then slower still.

And suddenly there it was! Not sort of, but exactly.

I was baffled; so if you slow the crop circle sound way down, you get the sound I heard over my cabin?

The next night, while scanning the skies through a night vision scope, I saw not just one but 2 UFOs, of a well known regional type known as Doughnuts. They actually looked like rings of light with centers that were darker then the surrounding sky. They performed arial maneuvers that kept me swinging the scope so I wouldn't loose them. Then I handed the scope to a local woman who was watching, curious. After a moment, she gasped and began following the craft herself, with great concentration. Finally she gave me back the scope.

"Que?" I asked her.

"Doughnut!" she replied.

It was probably inevitable that I should visit the Crop

131

Circles, eventually. The Pilgrim's path was leading me in that direction.

Every glyph I visited in England connected in it's symbol form to at least one another fringe experience, which occurred either years before or afterwards and far away from the fields of England.

The Koch fractal was probably #1.

For nearly a year before the Mexico trip I'd been 'getting' a design. 2 triangles, above and below, merging into a Star of David. In meditation, in dreams, I'd been drawing it, trying to figure out what it meant. It had to do with generation, I understood that. As in multiplying, reproduction.

During the night our plane set down in Heathrow, or the one following, a new fractal design appeared in the fields of Southern England next to Sillbury Hill. And we visited it two days later. The first of the Koch fractal sets, it described a 6 pointed star. Besides dividing into triangles, it was also podding like an amoeba into 6 smaller versions of itself, it's points morphing into even smaller stars. Which were podding, in turn, into dots representing even smaller stars. Expanding outward. Generating like a cluster of living crystals. When I walked into it it was like entering a temple. The glyph of my dreams---

Lurching back to the Mexico trip and the refrain that repeated in my head, 'Straight Circle Divide' ? 6 straight lines make up the circular form of the Star of David. There was my straight circle. A shape made still more circular by it's division into smaller stars, spreading on into infinity.

#2, the Torus, the first glyph we visited, was essentially an 'energy' doughnut. The synchronicity tied in with my craft sightings in Mexico. The object I'd followed---my first and only sighting of a UFO--- was doughnut shaped and even locally referred to as a Doughnut.

If the glyph had any message for me, what could it have been? And it's high voltage---or whatever the Hell it was---besides making me irritable, killed the batteries in my night vision. Which I'd tested only hours before to find full. What did that mean?

#3 The Circle and the Square. Crop Circles as viewed from a ziggurat?

When I visited England, I experienced 4 agriglyphs in all. The Koch set, (described) the Torus, and an odd 2 glyph set, made up of dissimilar but encircled designs. These actually stood a short walk away from each other but were set on the same 'line'.

As shown on my sketch, both designs were about the same size. But inside their 'rinds', they were entirely different.

One formed a circular swirl, turning from the center, implying energy and motion, the direction water might take, enclosed in a round form. The other was a grid work, resembling a sieve, suggesting stasis.

I met Colin Andrews later that week, breakfasting with his team at a local teahouse, and chatted about the latest formations. He suggested that there might be meaning in the seeming matched opposition of the pair. Which is when I started paying attention. Hadn't thought of that up till then.

About 3 years ago, I decided to get serious about learning ancient Sumerian cuneiform so I could study the earliest recorded creation stories for myself. After learning basic cuneiform designs and Sumerian phrases, I started working on phrases, and I thought it might be fun to try translating the term 'Crop Circle' into Cuneiform.

133

Symbols as Signposts?

4 Crop Circles;
Syncronicity
as communication
across time
and space?

The Doughnut Craft   **Torus**

The UFO I witnessed in Mexico was popularly known as a
Doughnut. Round and bright with a hole blacker then the night sky,
it returned to mind on entering my first crop circle in England.

My Mental Video   **Koch #1**

Merging triangles forming a Star of David. This has to do
with generation, I understood. The very first Fractal Koch Set
pattern was embedded within a day of our arrival in England.

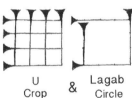

U   Lagab   **Grid & Wheel**
Crop & Circle

Transliterating the words Crop Circle into Sumerian
immediately brought to mind the 3rd and final crop circles I visited
in England. They were laid down close to each other
as though a set. Far right shows actual size cuneiform
would have been written on tablets.

134

After rendering the direct translation, 2 logograms, side by side, I sat staring at them for a moment, feeling baffled. What am I looking at? What am I missing? Then I drew a circle around the second symbol, the grid.

And the translated words for 'Crop Circle' expressed in Sumerian, although drastically reduced to the most simple of symbols---suggested the same matched set of crop circles that I'd visited nearly 20 years ago.

So am I implying that someone somehow knew I'd be studying Sumerian back then and plopped those 2 into the field simply for my personal benefit; knowing I'd stumble through them? Just to make me wonder years later, during this cuneiform translation??

Of course not; it's way deeper then that. It's not about me, it's about all of us and all at once, which makes it even more amazing. Because it seems a constant to this mystery, that the deeper you go, the deeper it gets. And the wider the roots spread and interconnect. If it was time for someone to notice the connection, it probably wouldn't matter who figured it out; it would happen regardless, it's just part of the tangle.

During the England visit, one thing that always gave me a quiet thrill whenever we'd visit a crop circle site, was spotting my crop circle pendants riding on the necks of other passing Pilgrims. Odds were good that they bought them from me at the Faire way back in California. Maybe even back then they were feeling inspired to plan a pilgrimage to visit these temporary temples, themselves. Maybe our talk and their new medicine piece even helped to activate them in some obscure way.

What sudden changes in life's path did all these other pilgrims experience once they'd returned home? What new synchros provided sign posts? When they connected with other pilgrims, in the fields, did they also experience a ramping up of synchros that continued after they'd separated and returned home?

Other Synchros from the Crop Circle Trip---as expected?

When our tour guide admitted she'd forgotten to book the promised over flights to view the crop circles, I was ready to start ripping out my hair. I'd bought a camcorder and brought my night vision just for that!

But then our rental van broke down and while we were waiting, Karen, a 'sister', showed up. We'd first met when we'd both rented sales tables at an LA UFO Congress. She was wearing the T shirt she'd created and was selling that year--- Hybrid Beings Unite! I was wearing mine--- Alien Spawn Unite! We'd pointed at each other and started laughing. Hung out whenever we ran into each other, which was suspiciously often, given that we lived on opposite coasts.

And so here she was, just happened to show up!

Although everyone knew all the pilots locally were booked solid on overflights months ahead of the crop circle season, being as she had a car and the van was stuck for a while anyway, we drove out to the airfield. Stopped the very first pilot walking by, who laughed incredulously when we asked him if he had any slots open during the next week. But at our persistent urging, he checked the little book in his pocket and was astonished to find out that in fact he did--- several hours worth in fact! Starting in only an hour, would we be ready?

Of course we were.

136

Valenya

Encounter # 3
I get my wish and I wish I didn't

After the first 2 visits, I began to wish, even mentally request, that I could be aware and awake just once, so I could know what was happening, what they did, who they really were?

Once again, it happened during a weekend I'd decided to stay home. I was feeling more then normally edgy and depressed, but I hadn't yet learned to recognize what it meant. I just thought I must need some rest from Faire. So Ter went down alone.

I tried to work off my irritation by cutting berry bushes, but that didn't work. I was so nervous that I threw up dinner.

I'd lately been sleeping upstairs because of the heat. One room had lots of windows I could open, so I'd put together a make shift cot up there.

Although exhausted from berry chopping and jewelry manufacture, I was still too tense to fall asleep. So, all evening, I flipped and flopped back and forth in bed and tried to relax. I probably ate a whole bottle of 'Calms' over the first part of that night. It didn't help. For hours, I heard the mini grandfather clock downstairs chiming the hours, till well past midnight. Still alert and bone tired at the same time.

Finally, about 3 o'clock I started to relax. Just a bit. And then, all at once, everything changed. As if that was the trigger.

I really don't think I left the house or even the room in any physical manner. I wasn't sucked through a window, or beamed up to a ship. It was too sudden.

I was still lying flat on my back but I was somewhere else, as though reality had suddenly morphed all around me.

I was still lying on my back on something flat and narrow, like my bed. But I felt paralyzed, not only in the normal sense, but also resulting from the most intense fear I've ever experienced in my life. Even at the time, I recognized it as feeling artificially produced. There were forms moving at super speed all around me. They seemed about 4 feet high. Actually, I couldn't tell if they were moving real fast or if I'd been slowed way down. In any case, I couldn't make out their faces, they just looked like blurs off to my side. And I couldn't move.

They worked with a focus, their sense of purpose was strong.

Just as I realized what had happened, I thought "They've got me!" But in what seemed like less then 3 seconds I was released again. And I was right back in my bed in my house. Just that fast. And they were gone from my room.. But I could feel them congregated in a circle in the center room of the house, adjoining mine, waiting to be transferred to where ever they came from. And the fear paralysis was still holding me tight as a vise.

For several minutes I lay still, barely daring to breath. I was even too afraid to reach out and flip the switch on the lamp, only a couple of feet from my head.

Although I hadn't been hurt, it was the unframebility of the experience combined with the complete helplessness that terrified me. And, as I'd mention, they seemed to be able to inject fear artificially.

When the fear suddenly dissolved, I realized they must be gone. Now I could move enough to switch on the lamp next to my bed. The light helped. I still had to go through the next room to go downstairs and check on my dog. Visions of dog mutilations filled my head. I held my breath, swung open the door and let the light spill in to the next room. No one there. I padded downstairs. My sheltie Roo was snoring softly, sleeping soundly in her dog bed. The clock said 3 am. I went back upstairs, went to bed and lay there till dawn, thinking.

I asked for it. And I got it. And now that it's over, I'm glad I did. But I understand now why they might choose to knock us out first and I'm not sure it's such a bad idea. They probably don't have the luxury of time to slow down and hold our hands; they have a job to do. And the stress of interaction with them can't be good for our 'containers' either. Why prolong it?

In any case I never asked to be awake 'during' again.

Contact #4

Waking under the Crud Blanket
or Making Encounters work for You?

Terry was home this time. He'd just returned from Faire, and was still buzzing both from the energy and the long eight hour drive home. It was hard not to catch and I did. Then I foolishly had a coffee to catch up to his speed and realized I probably wouldn't sleep at all that night. I let Ter have the bed on the bottom story and decided to go upstairs and watch stars through my night vision scope instead. I could always use my camp bed later, if I found I could sleep.

Scoping is an especially relaxing activity for me. There's almost always something moving around in the sky. In my upstairs bed room there were large windows opening to the east and south. I watched a bobbling light travel overhead. Then, nothing to watch but stars.

Starting to feel drowsy, I lay down and read. But I couldn't get comfortable. The trouble my knees, they hurt like Hell and had been for quite a while. Nothing mysterious, I'd overworked them, carrying heavy objects. Probably wore out the cartilage. I'd doubted doctors could do more then prescribe analgesics so I'd held off dealing with them. But sometimes the pain made it hard to sleep. Even walking up the stairs to my room had lately become a challenge. I needed to hang onto the bannister. Considering that I'd always been able to hike around the mountain, wherever and whenever I felt like it, up till now, this really scared me. Had I totally screwed up my future life?

Even allowing that it was my own foolish fault that I was in this situation to begin with, earlier that day, I'd mentally begged for a healing. If I said I prayed to God or Spirit, I'd be lying. I begged the beings who appeared to be involved with me.

I knew they could hear me; they'd reacted before when I tried to connect through emotion. The stronger I felt it, the harder I begged them, the quicker they seemed to respond. I quietly cried, while I mentally demanded that they come out and heal me. If they wanted my help, they needed me to be mobile and healthy, I reasoned. So it was in their best interest to help me heal. Felt better after the cry, at least.

I flipped through a copy of Fate, still somewhat wound up and my knees aching. Still laying on top of the bed. It was stifling hot for one thing, mid September. But mostly because the loosely knitted afghan cover was pretty dirty and the idea of crawling under it filled me with revulsion. It tended to collect crumbs, for one thing, and also hadn't been washed in quite a while. In fact, since I never actually went underneath it, I'd tucked it in tightly all the way around the bed. You really had to tug on it hard to get it out. No reason to do that.

I crawled on top of the afghan, knees painfully grinding.

First I lay on one side, then on the other. Then over to my back, but that made my legs hurt even worse. Finally I drifted off.

I woke up the next morning, feeling as though I was

suffocating, stifled from the heat. Surprise! I was laying several blankets deep, directly underneath the crud blanket. Quickly, I scrambled out of bed. How disgusting! But how could it have happened? I would have certainly have remembered getting up and crawling underneath the blankets, if I'd needed to jerk the covers out to get into bed, as that would have taken some sustained effort. Even besides having no incentive to get under them to begin with. And I never ever walk in my sleep.

About three days later I noticed that one of my knees wasn't aching. Inside of 2 weeks both knees were functioning again to where I could walk without pain. I was even able to run for short bursts, something I'd started to doubt I'd ever be able to do again. Soon I was walking without any pain at all.

So what happened? Apparently someone heard me and decided to to arrange what I'd requested. And they needed to remove me from my bed to accomplish it. But why pull out all the sheets in order to put me underneath them on return? Maybe they forgot where I'd actually been lying and so put me where they nearly always find humans; underneath? Although it probably took them some work, pulling out those covers!

My Alien Interview

It started with my usual scary UFO dream. I was in town, visiting some other people and we were running from alien craft, which were gliding about, flying low over the houses. They were shooting beams of light along the ground, searching, searching---I was ducking from one persons porch to another's carport, but I couldn't seem to find anywhere to hide.

The craft were everywhere, I was getting exhausted. Stay out of that beam!

Then the scene abruptly changed and I woke up. Inside the dream.

I knew I couldn't be awake, because of the circumstances. I was standing outdoors in a huge warm Summer filled field. The sky was blue, the sun felt good. There was a line of houses maybe a half mile or more in the distance.

Standing before me was a youngish man, maybe in his early forties. Medium height, blond, good looking in sort of a flat faced way. Very Nordic. I understood he was an ET.

He was smiling in a friendly manner, as if waiting, and I understood that I'd just been given the opportunity to ask him some questions. I was finally getting my alien interview, the

143

one that I'd always asked for! I'm surprised I didn't wake up at that point just out of excitement.

I forgot so much of the conversation, even before it was over. In fact, the trickiest part was the over-information. I'd think a question and he'd think back an explanation too fast for my brain and way above my intellectual understanding. Kind of overwhelming.

But I remembered 3 major 'bites' of information, because I went over and over them just as I was waking up.

At one point he was describing their mode of travel. And I became exited, exclaiming out loud "So it's true!" You're not coming down at all! You're coming 'through'! He smiled his answer. Bingo!

The second bite had to do with the blue light. He drew my thoughts to the first part of my dream, furtively hiding from the light.

"I don't think you understand, that the light injects information." he informed me. That startled me. I'd assumed that it was trying to grab me and I felt a little embarrassed. He told me that it often shone on me when I was asleep, so I still received the benefit, even unknowing. That made me feel better.

The 3rd Bite had to do with their presence on Earth. He explained that they were stationed here in order to work with us, in fighting the environmental crisis we were creating and they weren't leaving until it was resolved. It was spoken like a promise, and I appreciated that. I could tell he wasn't lying. There was an odd mix of amusement and disgust in his 'voice' as he told me this. Exasperation?

Then I was dropped back into my previous 'dream'. Still hiding from the UFOs and their beams. I tried to talk to the other humans and explain what I'd just been told, but they either wouldn't believe me or were still too afraid of the craft.

144

They weren't interested in listening.
And then I woke up.

To find the sheets beneath me completely soaked in sweat, something I'd never experienced before. I was so exited, I could barely wait for Ter to wake up so I could tell him about it.

Was it a thank you for a UFO article I'd recently submitted for publication? How did they know how to create and control a virtual zone in my sleeping brain in order to provide a place for us to meet and to converse? And while I'm asking questions, was the Nordic even truly a Nordic? After all it could have just as easily been the cover image for a Gray or Mantis and I probably wouldn't know, considering they could also manufacture the virtual landscape we were standing in with such ease? Did it even have a physical form or was that also created for my benefit? Or does it even matter?

I guess all I have to go with was the feeling I got from the being. Kindness, love and unbelievable intelligence. There's some things you just can't fake.

The Spectral Tree Stump

Our neighbors Raymond and Nancy first saw the apparition several weeks after the forest was cut down. The logging was due to a contract made by Raymond's departed father as a gift to his new wife. She had the right to harvest.

An out of the ordinary event ensued when she elected to cut timber outside of the tree farm. Older stately conifers on the periphery of the tree farm were cut down. According to local lore, the giant firs had defined an Indian burial ground.

Raymond and Nancy live in a wooden castle they built by themselves, nestled into the forest, on top of a rocky knob. The castle has two towers and rises 5 stories high---nearly as tall as the surrounding conifers and massive oaks. Their property connects to his stepmother's land.

At night and in the evening, the shadows of the trees play across the driveway and lawn. Which is probably why they took a while to notice the dark apparition.

Their circular driveway provided a convenient track for a short run and Raymond liked to follow it for a lap or 2 in the evening, just before dark. During one such run, a large dark form caught his eye. Hovering in the air a few yards off the driveway, it was approximately four feet tall and four and a half feet high and shaped very much like a tree stump. He could easily see underneath it as it seemed to be hovering about two feet off the ground. It wasn't transparent or filmy like a traditional spirit but rather an opaque black. It didn't

146

seem to be threatening him; however it was odd in that it could defy gravity.

After puzzling over it for a bit, he continued his run. Nancy was also watching from an upstairs window and she noticed that the black apparition was now following behind Raymond by a small distance, though he was not aware of it. When she told him about it later, Raymond began to suspect that it wanted to tell him something. But what?

The apparition's shape and the timing of it's arrival made him think it might be connected to the logging incident. But what was it, exactly? The Spirit of the forest that had been cut? Or something to do with the older growth of fir that Raymond had enjoyed, simply because they were majestic and he had climbed them in the past?

As you may have surmised, neither Raymond or Nancy felt especially threatened by their visitor. Nancy is highly sensitive in the way of spirits and has had enough experience with them not to be easily 'spooked'. Raymond is not quite as sensitive, but has a personality leaning more towards friendly curiosity then fear. If it wanted to be there it was welcome, as far as he was concerned.

Which was good, because it now began to accompany Raymond on his evening runs, waiting for him at the spot in their driveway, where the pipe that brought in their spring water crossed it. As Raymond ran by, the apparition would fall in line, gliding a short distance behind him.

A few days after the new development, Raymond's cousin Sudi visited from Florida and Raymond had the grand idea to share his experience with his beautiful cousin.

"I invited my wife and cousin for a walk around the loop and of course was disappointed that my black apparition was not present. On our third lap around the driveway, to my delight, I saw the hovering shape about 25 feet up our adjacent well road.

All three of us stopped. I pointed to it and asked my two witnesses if they saw my black apparition, for it was floating in the middle of the road. We all agreed, yes, it was black. It was in the dark of the evening, it was even darker; it was hovering, not moving, approximately two feet off the ground and it looked like a tree stump with just a few roots.

I was so elated that it had decided to show up, that I told the girls that I was going to meet it. It was approximately 25 feet away and I set off to investigate. I was so interested in what it might be that I walked right up to it and with my

148

next step I would have stepped through it. However that is not what happened.

For at that same second, I was suddenly standing between the two girls who had not budged from their observation point 25 feet away. I had traveled the twenty five feet backwards in the blink of an eye. I was exited---,thrilled---; I turned to the girls and said "Did you see that?"

"Yes, and we are going in the house!"

The apparition had not hurt me; I had not felt a thing. I know I moved, but not with my feet. It was amazing and I could not leave with the girls. Instead I stayed...right there, and I guess I felt I owed it an explanation. It looked like a tree stump, so I explained that the trees that I was responsible for were valued for their beauty, their magic, and that any harvests and firewood gatherings would be conservative and mindful of preservation. I felt at peace with the apparition and left it hovering there, and rejoined the girls in the house."

A post script to this story was added months later, when a friend of Raymond's visited a psychic and had him come along. He urged Raymond to tell her about his apparition. Raymond's friend had already told her enough that she asked Raymond to give her the whole story. She confirmed that it was the spirit of a Native American and that a burial ground had been disturbed.

The black apparition has not returned.

But there's something else I should probably add.

In Portland, Oregon two young women out walking in the woods, also came upon a hovering tree stump, and in broad daylight as well. So there's two reports of these things.

Unlike our neighbor's Shadow Stump, however, this one

was shiny, light and rainbow hued. The women beat a rapid retreat. I wonder if it jogged along behind them?

I also wonder if it might be the same sort of being, as the Shadow, only seen in full daylight? Just a thought. But wasn't it odd that the Rainbow Stump was witnessed only some 40 miles away from Raymond's Shadow?

Contact in Canada

At the end of my articles, I often liked to tag on an invitation to share any strange stories readers might have had. Experiences that share elements of my own especially interest me; what do the constellations of common elements suggest? Patterns point to meaning.

Following my experiences with the 'Sounding', I've also been listening for other reports that connect UFOs with sounds.

Aren't UFOs supposed to be noiseless? So I've read, but I've personally heard reports of exceptions to this rule. And what's very interesting is that there seem to be several consistent kinds of sounds reported. Sometimes you just hear one sound. Not infrequently you might hear several, overlapping each other, like I did with my road grader.

Susanna, my corespondent, had also heard one of the sound themes, and not only once but twice in her life. Both accompanied with a UFO.

In reading Susanna's e mail correspondence, I was also intrigued by the number of elements we shared as experiencers. Not only the sounds, but the scoop marks that appeared to be connected. The strange disturbing spirits she encountered in her parental home. Even the fact that our

151

experiences happened mainly on Reservation land, (in Canada called the Reserve) though we lived half a continent apart.

She'd contacted me originally to share an experience she'd had at the age of 14, while living in her Grandparents home on the 6 Nation's Reserve. She was upstairs doing homework when she heard a car pull up. Then a car door slammed and a moment later someone walked up onto the porch and into the living room. She heard both doors close. Then the steps proceeded on into the kitchen.

Glad someone was home, she came downstairs to greet them. No one was there. No car parked on the drive, no boot prints on the floor. But the cat was sitting on the stool, staring at her and his eyes were huge.

Susanna walked into the kitchen and said "Hello!" No answer. The light wasn't on. The cat was still staring at her.

This disturbed her so much, that she went right back upstairs and turned the television up---loud! When a car finally did pull up, she got a good look at it through the window before coming down.

Nice to have the cat to serve as a witness that something strange had happened! I think of my dogs barking at the 'plane' sound that morphed into my 'Road Grader" when it passed overhead. Animals can't talk about it but they know when something isn't right. At least it's confirmation that it's not just you!

Pondering such an interesting account, I couldn't help asking her if she'd experienced other strange happenings in that house?

Apparently so and not just on the bottom story. Susanna recalled several times that she'd heard people come up the staircase when she was upstairs, but there was no one there.

152

One time when she was in her room, lying on her bed, taking a nap, she heard someone come in and a hand touched her face, twice. When she struck out against it, there was no one there.

When I asked about the history of the house, might it have been haunted? she replied that her grandparents had never told her anything about it, because they believed in many kinds of supernatural beings and didn't talk about things like that, feeling that would encourage them. Growing up, they'd been told about shape shifters, witch lights, ghosts and devils.

Susanna herself had seen the witch lights as a child, but never got close enough to see what they were. She said that the lights looked like a person's aura, except really strong and intensely colored. Once she'd seen such a witch fall from the top of a pine tree.

She doesn't see them anymore, though. Her father explained that it's because the old ones died and the new ones don't know what the old ones did.

Another odd parallel of experience---when Ter and I moved into the mountains of Kings Valley our neighbor asked if we'd seen the colored lights up the creek behind our house. Never did, though I looked for them.

Also, I was very interested to learn that way over in Ontario, the first Nations had much the same Bigfoot traditions as those in Northern California, especially in regards to there being 3 separate kinds, each with the same descriptions as ours! That kind of consistency in understanding and reports, although separated by thousands of miles makes it hard not to take seriously.

Then Susanna told me about her experience with the

sounding. It happened during the Summer of '91' when along with her two sisters and baby brother, she was visiting her Dad on the Six Nations of the Grand River. It was night time and she was watching a movie on the T.V.

The television sat by the patio window and the curtains were drawn open. She noticed lights up in the sky but assumed they were from an airplane, since their house was situated on a flight path to the airport. So she went back to watching the movie. But about an hour later Susanna felt very funny. Looking out the window, she could see that the lights hadn't moved. Realizing it couldn't be a plane or helicopter she called her dad. At this moment the lights took off.

So she went back to her movie. About two hours later she felt strange again, and looked out the window. The lights were back. Again she called for her dad. Again the lights took off, but in a different direction then before.

Some time after her dad and brother went to bed, she and her sisters followed suit.

"We were laying in bed, laughing and joking, when there was a noise that sounded like a huge engine above the house. Now we live so far back from the road that it wasn't possible for someone to be there. The noise got louder and louder and it got bright in our room and then our dad was trying to wake us up."

Four months later, Susanna noticed marks on the corners of her eyes. It looked like she'd been burnt. Also there was a circle at the end of a cut up towards her temples. This was not something she'd been born with, she emphasized. Over time it faded.

She was to hear the sound once again. This time it happened in Tampa, Florida. There were pink fluffy clouds in the sky, so she couldn't see the source, but only hear the noise. A lady parked her car nearby and asked her what the noise was? It lasted for 5 minutes then faded away. Once it was gone, so were the fluffy pink clouds.

When I thanked Susanna for taking the time to share her experiences, she said she was more then happy to share them; being of a curious mind, she had many questions herself!

Her sounding resembled that of an overhead engine, not a road grader. But the round skin markings that resulted made an interesting overlap with my experience. She told me a few other things that also made me take note.

When lying on a pillow, in her room, she'd heard music that made her wonder if the neighbors were having a party? But when she opened the window, it was silent outside. When she lay down again, the music resumed. Her Grandmother told her she was hearing the music from Hell. More overlap with my voices heard while falling asleep?

Unrelated to the rest of this report, but very interesting on it's own, was an experience her Grandfather had once had with a Shape shifter.

There was an old man who lived down the road, who used to visit them. Her grandfather had lately been noticing meat going missing from the drying house. When it continued, he decided to wait and catch whoever was doing it.

"In the middle of the night, a big pig came into the yard and right up to the drying house. My Grandfather shot the pig in the right side of it's face.

My Grandma said it was about a month later that the old man came to visit, after not showing up to visit for so long. She said when he showed up, he had a bandana covering the right side of his face. I think it made my Grandpa mad, because he had shown the hospitality that we are raised on and this man had taken and still came back and stole more."

The wounded Shape shifter that betrays his guilt by revealing a similar wound in his human form, what a universal theme!

As Dog is my Witness

I like to get up at 5, study cuneiform and listen to podcasts till dawn.

So it's still plenty dark when I let out the dogs to relieve themselves, and I enjoy the stars, while I wait, visibility permitting.

This morning, Jasper walked out, looked up and growled, his hackles rising. He was on high alert, warning me about something that troubled him.

I looked too, but couldn't see a thing moving, though the sky was clear. I could have gone inside for my glasses or night vision scope, but I knew I didn't really need to. Jasper is always right. Somewhere way up there was a tiny pinprick of light, crossing the sky.

Aren't dogs supposed to be sight challenged? I doubt he can smell whatever's up there. I've pointed out Jasper's ability to visiting friends and they concur. Those with 20 20 sight can barely pick up what my dog can. And he takes it really personally as to what's intruding on his skies!

I've always wondered whether there could be some tie in to those dancing dimes on the ceiling?

I appreciate my dog for being present for that incident and for alerting me to it to begin with.

It was September, Terry was down state working at the

Renaissance Faire, and I'd been sleeping upstairs in the guest room, taking advantage of the only cool place in the house. Jasper slept at the foot of the bed.

Although there were windows on 3 sides of the room, they opened into tall thick fir forest. Our nearest neighbors lived on a dirt road about a mile down from our house, past a locked gate, standing about halfway between their house and ours. No one lived above us, the road was blocked by fallen timber. The guest room had only 2 electrical outlets. There was nothing plugged into them, but a bedside light, which was turned off.

Sometime very early in the morning, maybe two or three A.M., I awoke to feel Jasper shifting about on the bed. He was sitting up and moving his head and shoulders to keep careful watch over what appeared to be a number of perfectly round, dime to quarter sized circles of intensely bright light, which were swirling on the ceiling above us. They seemed to be dancing, and moving inside a circumference of maybe 4 feet, mid ceiling, right over Jasper and my feet. They felt as if they might possibly be intelligently controlled.

We watched them intently, but that's all they did. Swirled around and around each other, like skaters at the Ice Capades. After a while, they seemed to fade out. Jasper sighed and lay down and went back to sleep. I got up and looked out the windows. No house lights visible any closer then 15 miles away, far down the river.

There had been no beams, like a flashlight would make to suggest a point of origin. Just bright round autonomous lights sliding across the ceiling. Really, only a bank of tiny flashlights on my bed all pointing straight up and revolving all at once could have created any display like that, to show only round lights, rather then elliptical.

The next night I woke up once again, at probably about

the same time. Again, Jasper was sitting up, head pointed at the ceiling. But there was nothing there---that I could see, at any rate. Either the show had just ended before I awoke, or he could see things I couldn't.

Dogs as witness's can be a mixed blessing. They can't confirm their sightings to humans who weren't there, only to those who were. And then they bark when they get exited. Noise pollution or validation or both?

I heard the 'Road Grader' sound a second time, maybe two years after the first, early on a foggy autumn evening. It was just after twilight, when our 2 dogs and I heard a very slow plane coming in from the East. It was flying so slow as to be very disturbing. It just seemed that at that speed it would have to drop and crash before long. I tensed up, listening. So did the dogs; you could tell that they both sensed that the sound wasn't 'right'. Still, the plane somehow remained aloft.

But just before it passed over head, the sound shifted. There was an overlap as the slow plane drone morphed into the Road Grader grind.

The dogs immediately started barking at full volume in response. I ran outside into darkening fog, followed by dogs, still barking. Yelling "Shut Up!" which of course made them more even exited and they barked louder still. I couldn't see a thing through the fog. When the dogs had finally subsided, I could only hear a familiar too slow plane, now far to the west and fading.

The Exploding Living Room. I'm glad Terry was there for the second time this happened. Not just the dogs. It's nice to have human confirmation as well. They can talk about it with you and compare notes.

It happened in the exact middle of the living room, twice in a row.

The first time there was only me and the 2 dogs, Jasper and a German Shepherd named Shadow. I was sitting, reading at the window, at the north west end of the living room and the dogs were lying down in the north east corner. Suddenly, a sound exactly like a bullet splintering glass exploded, but at something like five times amplification, launching me straight out of my chair. The three of us abruptly turned to stare at the middle of the room. At nothing.

Although I searched about, in the attic and under the floor, both above and below 'ground zero' I could never find anything to account for it.

2 years later the living room exploded again. In the

same spot, but a completely different explosion.

This time, both Terry and I were sitting next to his computer, in an adjacent room, which was separated from the living room by an arch, no door. We had a very good view of the living room.

The best comparison for the sound we heard would be if someone dropped a small horse, maybe a 800, 1000 pounder, from a distance of about twice the distance of the ceiling to the floor. It sounded heavy enough to go right through the floor when it hit.

This time Ter and I both jumped. And the dogs, who were resting near our chairs, jumped too. All four of us stared at the middle of the living room. But there was nothing. Again. This time Ter and I both looked over and under the house. It happened in the very middle of the room, we both agreed.

We moved away from that area about a year ago. We got to know the buyers a bit before we left and visit them sometimes. I keep meaning to ask them whether their living room has exploded yet?

Kate's Story

I met Kate many years ago, online. A Montana lady, we got on well right from the start, e-mailing often over earth mysteries, crop circles and UFOs. More then once I asked her if she'd ever had any interaction with ETs? When she finally asked why I believed she might, I observed that she only reminded me of every Experiencer I'd ever met. If I was to pull out my 'Cowbird' list, I'd have checked every box. I've noticed that with Experiencer friends we often tend to find areas of 'overlap'. In her case, her Ukrainian ancestors, and her mate, who was also a tall craftsman named Terry.

Kate is what is known as a Dreaming Woman in many Native traditions. She's had so many precognitive dreams that she wrote down and collected a book of them for her kids. A book she also shared with me.

My personal favorite was the dream of falling snowflakes she'd had, when she was camping in Montana during the Summer. She awoke to find out that Mt. Saint Helens had just erupted in the state of Washington next door, and big fluffy ashes were already drifting down!

One dream in particular grabbed me right away. To me, it seemed nothing less then a warning from ETs. I realize that dreams are considered iffy as confirmation of contact--- but what do you think?

Ever since my Alien Interview, I listen to people's stories

of dream contact. It's often occurred to me that the reason Kate doesn't remember any physical ET contact could be because she doesn't need it. She's sufficiently intuitive that they can get through to her in more cost effective ways. Why give her training wheels she doesn't need? Why waste the gas or fusion when they can simply visit her in her mind?

She tells this story much better then I could---

"May 19, 1997

As a young freshman student, I took a job working for the Montana Department of Fish and Game. During the Fall and Winter, I worked in the Department of Film for Mr. Tom Warren, cleaning and repairing department films that were loaned out to various organizations and schools. We operated like a library. During the Summer I worked under the direction of Mr. Vince Yannone, caring for hurt or orphaned animals. We would receive fawns, bear cubs, antelope babies, a badger pair that were pretty scary and various birds including hawks, eagles, pelicans, anything hikers and campers found hurt or abandoned in the wild. Caring for the animals, I would work either a night shift at 11;00 P.M. or the morning shift at 7;00 A.M. My partner and I would switch off, taking turns at both feeding times, the afternoon shift we both covered.

I began getting phone calls at home, no one would speak! Usually I would just hang up. Then I began to notice pieces of the vine that grew on the fence cut and lying inside the animals cages. The vine was in an area that could not be reached by the animals. At night I had the feeling I was being watched. There was no phone for us to use in the animal center. I was feeling uncomfortable going to the compound at night. Then I had the dream!

163

The Dream

I dreamed I went to the compound to feed the animals. I walked in and the baby deer had vertical slashes all over their faces. Not enough to kill them but enough to make them bleed a lot. I looked to my left, through the cages and saw a space ship. I felt immediate anger, thinking that the space people had done this. I heard a voice from within the ship saying "We didn't do this, we are here to warn you...LOOK!"

Quickly, I looked down the long compound, with cages on either side and animals in nearly every one. The fawns had free run in the middle and access to the yard outside. I saw a full grown cougar on top of the cages to the left. My thoughts were immediate, "Cougar, don't kill the deer, and where will I be safe?"

I opened a cage door on the right that was empty in between the bears and crawled in. I knew that if I had to sit there all night till someone came in the morning I would be safe. The mountain lion jumped in one leap across the compound to the top of the cage I was in. I looked up at the deadly claws! He growled! Suddenly his paws turned into a man's hands with black leather gloves holding a switch blade! I started to look at his face. I was terrified and woke up before I saw it.

Reality. Now, upon waking, I realized that I definitely needed to pay attention! The phone quit working at our house. My roommates and I called the phone company from the neighbor's. A man came out to repair the trouble and told us that the wire had been cut on the pole and that no one else's was, just ours! Shortly after, my partner called from the morning shift, "Get down here, you have to see this." Every one was there, my boss Vince, an Indian fellow that worked as a warden and half a dozen others.

The deer had been cut exactly like my dream, there was blood smeared all over the kitchen walls and door, at the entrance of the compound. It looked like a hand did it! Vince said "Maybe an owl did it?" I didn't buy that for a minute. I told every one of my dream!! My partner started taking her boyfriend on the night shift. I borrowed a german shepherd dog named Buck who was trained to attack on command from a night watchman at Bailey's insulation Warehouse. My room mates and I all decided to move. We went in three different directions. Eventually the phone calls stopped, then resumed years later. I enrolled in Karate class."

About that warning; interesting that the ETs replied to Kate's thought accusations as easily as if she was speaking out loud. And that they realized she might assume the violence was their doing, unless they set her straight.

Kate has had other dreams of UFOs.

Still I was a little surprised when it was Kate who nudged me into attending Experiencers Speak #4, a conference created by and for experiencers. But she was bound to go and I wasn't about to be left behind---

Experiencers Speak. And We Listen---

Is there any other area of study besides UFO/ human involvement where the closer you stand to the subject, the less credibility you inspire--- not only in the area of UFOs but in your sanity as well? No wonder that until recently, most Experiencers buffered their stories through experts who actually wrote the books and left them anonymous. And how many of those researchers slanted the stories and trimmed off the loose ends to make them more believable and thus protect their own reputation? Probably quite a few. It's just human nature.

"I can't afford to tell the truth, I have my credibility to protect!" That is the paradox.

Maybe you attend UFO Congresses so you can find out what's really going on. Until recently you didn't talk too loudly about your personal experiences even there. In a field where credibility is hard enough to come by, experts may want to keep the really controversial stuff at arms length. You're kind of like the crazy uncle who comes to the family reunion. At least, it was like that 20 years ago.

Things have changed. Now there's Experiencers Speak, thanks to Audrey Starborn, a conference brought about by and for the people who have experienced contact

It's funny how people tend to play leap frog with each

166

other. When I aroused an interest in Kate to find out if she was involved, she pried me out of my armchair to attend Experiencers Speak. And I've been blessing her for that ever since.

Flying from Portland Oregon to Portland Maine, coast to coast, I brought my UFO and agriglyph jewelry and rented a sales table inside the presentation room, in order to cut travel costs while still taking in every talk. Plus it's always nice to have a home base, a place for people to linger and visit.

Besides interacting with others of my 'tribe' there were certain things I specifically wanted to find out more about.

The issue of communality of contact experience was of special interest to me. I was curious if there were more common traits then I'd recognized myself, thus far. Kathleen Marden, the niece of Betty Hill and an experiencer herself, had done a great deal of study on just this subject.

The Shamanic /UFO experience overlap. Mike Clelland's presentation would be covering that as well as synchronicitys concerning certain animals, especially owls.

Nancy duTertre, an attorney and police psychic detective, was sharing her research in the area of exolinguistics, alien communication, another favorite subject of mine. Are they speaking to us and if so how? And how can we answer?

Jim Weiner was reflecting on his experiences as one of the Allagash 4, he and 3 friends who had been abducted as a group, while camping. I was curious how he viewed the experience, from the perspective of several decades after the event. I was also hoping to ask him about all those twins? Because the field seems top heavy with them.

The 'Meet and Greet' was held at the Cryptozoology

Museum, created and run by Loren Coleman, an eminent cryptozoologist. You couldn't start off any better then that. A full size bigfoot statue stood just inside the door. I was careful to buy a pile of Coelacanth T shirts (great artwork!) for the folks back home.

I've noticed that synchronicitys tend to occur following not only UFO experiences but visits with other experiencers as well. That being so, I wondered if this event would work in similar fashion, only on steroids?! Two full days of talking to no one else but other experiencers? And it did; I experienced synchros back to back. Even down to a book I'd picked up pre conference, intending to tone down with it at night, after the talks. Valis, by Philip K Dick. I started reading it the night before.

I read about the protagonist of the novel being hit by a ray of light , which upgraded his mind. A classic Experiencer story unfolded, complete with many of the same commonalities I'd be hearing about for the next 2 days. Not only did the hero believe he was dealing with ETs but he kept philosophizing about the primordial twins of mythology.

It turns out this was a thinly disguised autobiography. When I read his author's bio, I was not at all surprised to find out he was a twin, whose sister had died at birth. Just one more synchronicity for the conference---

It was a rich two days. There were many speakers and not a one worth missing. Some like Stanton Friedman were especially well known. His presentation would convince anyone with half a brain, that, yes, UFOs are with us and the Government has known about it forever; blatantly offering obvious lies and blockage, and sometimes causing serious injury.

Bill Konkoleski, Michigan State Director for Mufon, riffed off his personal history, sharing many puzzling incidents that his listeners could recognize and relate to. My favorite take away was his story regarding a special translucent green stone called moldavaite. As a young man he felt drawn to buy a sample of this meteor. Which promptly disappeared. He bought another, but the same thing happened again! And since he'd begun sharing his story, he'd had other folks tell him similar stories. An interesting postscript is that since the Ex. Speak conference, one of the other presenters, completely unknown to him, has also blogged about having the same experience.

Thomas Reed presented on his families experiences with the 'visitors', as well as his own personal retained memories. An interesting aside is that since the conference, he's managed to get an impressive historical monument set in place in his home town, commemorating the group abduction and treating it as an actual physical event. That has to be a first!

Peter Robbins was master of ceremonies, handling lumps like no shows and over runs with grace and humor.

I thought it interesting that during her presentation about ET communication, Nancy du Tertre suggested that synchronicitys might be considered one form of messaging from ET to Experiencer. It certainly resonated with the stories I'd heard from other Experiencers. Her presentation also compared forms of ancient writing to samples said to be channeled or received from ET entities. Comparing the systems on the screen was fascinating. The earliest Sumerian cuneiform struck me as especially elegant and possibly ET inspired.

Reflecting on his famous group abduction story, Jim Weiner made a point about one curious and consistent reaction to UFO contact---artistic ability. Each of the 4 men abducted in the famous Allagash case already had some artistic ability beforehand, but their abilities exploded in the years following. Weiner himself teaches art at a university. He presented artwork done by each of the participants, rendered before and after the experience. The difference was staggering. He noticed that his own ability gained a more organic quality, resulting from insights he gained about nature and process, that he felt resulted from his interaction.

The Experiencer's Commonalities aspect was covered by Kathleen Marden, who has been compiling an in depth study for years. She shared a long list that was often surprising. For example, one trait is a taste for salty snacks over sweet!

An obvious Shamanic overlap was touched on by many speakers during the conference, but especially Mike Clelland. You could not help but consider that four hundred years ago, in some parts of the world, an experiencer would have had a cultural framework to hang his/her experiences on and a social identity or even a vocation to to go along with it. Now they're treated with uneasy toleration at best.

More then a few speakers mentioned the baffling prevalence of twins. The conference promoter/creator was a twin as well as 2 of the presenters. When I asked Jim Weiner at the end of the conference if he'd noticed an over abundance of twins in the field, he answered emphatically yes. An interesting point he shared was that it wasn't until he'd mentioned to Ray Fowler, who researched the Allagash case, that he was a twin, that he got his attention. Fowler had noticed the abundance of twins even way back then and was already curious about this puzzle.

By the end of the conference, Kate was convinced. She'd recognized the event as a stealth family reunion right away- her own! I felt pretty much the same. When the conference finally finished, which was well past Midnight on Sunday, as many hugs as business cards were exchanged.

Directly following the conference, I finally signed up with Facebook in order to keep up with the people I'd just met. It was a very satisfying thing to discover and connect with your tribe and I didn't want to risk loosing contact! Later, over facebook the interactions spawned more synchronicitys. This was an unexpected but very welcome byproduct!

About a month after the conference, I began getting inspirations for a series of block prints following years of inspirational log jam. The ideas flowed effortlessly, like water. I'd forgotten about this part of Jim Weiner's talk!

Also, nudged by Nancy du Tertre's presentation, I gave in to an inspiration to learn Sumerian so I could decide for myself what our earliest written history implied in the way of ET involvement.

Now, three years later, I'm transliterating psalms and myths, comparing interpretations and thoroughly enjoying the process. Nothing I'd previously have believed I'd ever be doing; since I was always pretty hopeless at languages previously. It was worth it, the compulsion produced a reply.

Recently I finished working out the Lamentation for the destruction of Ur, simply taking the Sumerians at their word. Nowhere in this work is there any mention either of armies or of battles. The fire comes down from heaven at the order of the 'top Boss' in the sky, after the lesser bosses unsuccessfully try to talk him out of it. The 'evil wind' spews fire and poison, people fall sick and die and the city is destroyed.

Yet this Liturgy has always been interpreted as invasion by outside armies. We simply had no other framework until recently to see it any other way.

It seems obvious that not only are the visitors here now, but they've been here since before writing began. We've feared and worshipped them as Gods in the past. But we've evolved quite a bit since then.

And now, judging from what I gleaned off the conference, it even appears that they may be trying to communicate with us! Maybe we're nearing the time when we can meet them on level ground?

Cowbird Chicks Part 2
Naming the The Constellations

It's interesting to note that if you interface with ETs you're also more likely to have had sightings of ghosts, Bigfoot, and other bizarre beings. Right up there in commonalities.

At a UFO conference in San Francisco, one well dressed, professional type, who introduced himself as a psychologist, stopped at the table to tell me all about a huge bird with a specked belly he'd witnessed in the Southwest. "I saw the Thunderbird!" he asserted; emphatically, referring to the legendary monster of the Native people of the Southwest. He was convinced that they were right and that the bird was non fictitious. I'd already given him a quick evaluation along cowbird lines, and found a perfect line up, so his crypto-critter story just trimmed things out. Our Hupa friend who found those Bigfoot prints and squat was also semi famous by his friends for being a UFO magnet. "Just hang around this guy, you'll see them." They all had.

Do we see the whole spectrum of crypto beings if we see a corner? The whole zoo or nothing? And what does this mean? This one has me baffled.

Also you're more likely to be psychic.

Chicken or egg? Were we this way before our 1st encounter or before birth? Was it an engineered factor in our physical package? Or was it simply what attracted the visitors and if so why? One thing everyone notices, if they've been paying attention, is that Experiencers often gain a level in ability following encounters, sometimes temporarily but not always. For myself, I've noticed a spike directly afterwards, that seems to settle at a level somewhere above where it was previously.

My wager is that it's a matter of upgrade, intended to facilitate communication with the visitors in the future. And with each other. Until we develop a more functional manner of communication, we can't go forward.

Look at it this way.

They've already tried everything else, seldom with rewarding results.

If they land the craft, people either run away or attack them. And the fear humans emit blocks any psychic communication they might attempt with us. It's like a wall.

They can hold us down with fear-paralysis but then again, we're too stunned to hear them.

They can insert a lucid dream, but unless they fling a fat bat against our window immediately afterwards to wake us up---Fast!--- we'll probably forget it all by morning. And if we do remember it, we'll probably discount it anyway.

Fling a fat bat. They did that with me, once, right after a dream filled with cryptic messages and images. It worked, I just about jumped, as it whacked the glass right behind my head. Flying against the window, it whacked it at least three times before leaving. Oddly it was a species of bat I'd never seen before, one way larger then the ones I was familiar with.

174

Because it produced more noise, hitting the glass?

Our spoken language is clunky, extremely subjective and arbitrary, ESP may not be the perfect substitute but it's probably way more functional.

As an aside, I've noticed that using this, you can call them in to request a healing. Or anything else, it appears. I'm always surprised by what they can pull off. Just find a place to be alone and direct your wish toward them, riding on heartfelt emotion. "Please do this for me." Then wait. They don't even seem to need to be around at the time you ask.

Maybe the upgrade's not such a bad thing. They say they're doing it for us. Maybe we just haven't considered how to fully take advantage of it yet.

Unexplained sounds will take place near you.

Explosions are normal. As mentioned, we've had 2 of these already in our old home. Always in the same place, center of the living room. One clue? A lady I knew who ran a UFO tour group said she'd heard 'my' road grader sound herself, in Puerto Rico inside the family home of a Hybrid, a woman who actually looked like she might be half ET, pointed chin, impossibly slim body. The sound issued from the same spot in the house where the ETs would usually manifest when they visited. She saw it as some sort of a station. Was the 'road grader' the sound of a door closing?

If you live next door to or on top of these entrances, does this suggest that they might move Experiencers from one living location to the next, for their own convenience in dealing with us? It would be expedient. Was that a door in our living room as well?

Something I should probably also mention about my explosions as it might be important. Both times when these occurred, I was thinking about paranormal science writers I really needed to contact regarding articles I was writing about crop circles and UFOs. I'd been dragging my heels. And I got right on it, afterwards, too. More puzzling Synchros?

You can expect impossible and baffling messages through voice media set up in an apparently choreographed manner.

Once, during a visit to my brother's house, he loaned me a book, called Silent Invasion. It was especially focused on the Hudson Bay sightings of the mid eighties and was researched and written by an experiencer by the name of Ellen Crystal. I was told that the book was already due at the library so I read it that night while 'sleeping' on the couch. Dropped it into the book slot in the Willow Creek branch on the way back home. Then spent the last hours drive thinking.

Besides the sightings she'd mentioned, I was surprised I hadn't known that big outdoor Rock concerts tended to draw UFOs and certain bands more then others. It made me think of a song by Neil Young I always liked and used to play on the guitar; After the Gold Rush. It seemed to end with a mass contact taking place and I wondered what inspired Mr. Young to write it? Also, I realized I'd forgotten some of the words and that bothered me, because I suddenly felt like playing it.

When I got home I was still buzzy from town, so I thought I'd engrave some crop circle pendants for Faire and listen to the local Hupa Native radio station to decompress.

It was just after noon and they were finishing up with National Native News. Then they always went into an hour of Native American music, both traditional as well as more pop or pow wow based. Only Indian, however, that was the rule.

They kicked it off with a humorous song about a young

guy trying to get to a pow wow in a crumbling Res rocket, hoping the eagle feather hanging from the dashboard would power him through.

Then the song faded out and guess what came on next? The first bars were unmistakable.

I had a pencil in hand within moments and started scribbling the forgotten lines on the surface of my wooden work bench. When the song ended it segued into the next song, this time a Native American, song.

What just happened?

If it was all happening in my mind, how could that have occurred? And the missing lines, how convenient; given within minutes of my sitting down! The funny thing was I'd felt almost anticipatory right before it happened. As if I was waiting---

At this time there was no phone service in our area. I really wanted to call up the DJ and ask what possessed him? To insert a non native song into the line up at that particular point in time? And what if he said he hadn't? Because it had followed the song before and preceded the next one so seamlessly, just the way they set them up at the station to prevent dead air.

You will see strange lights.

Maybe pulsing lights outside the window. Maybe colored lights in the woods. Maybe orbs or beams of various hues. Craft may be shiny and bright. Beings too.

If you do not recognize your connection early in life, you will probably catch on around middle age. How many long term UFO Researchers suddenly remember their own life long involvement, once they hit about 45 or so? As well, often enough, as the involvement of their families.

I'm sure the ETs know by now how consistently humans squeeze out those individuals whose experiences frighten their herd. No matter what they select or hybridize us for, we're still a social critter. As long as we don't know we're different we'll probably be tolerated. Once we're established financially or otherwise and our life long interest in UFOs has been validated and we have some understanding, then they can let us access our own back files and that way no one goes nuts or broke. Seems like an intelligent system to me---

Oddly, I've noticed more youngsters catching on earlier and seeming less stressed by it. Because it's embedded as a meme in our culture and they have a framework to put it in? Yeah, I'm a Hybrid; so what?

I look at that as encouraging.

Oh; and it certainly doesn't seem to hurt if you happen to be a twin. I wonder if twins suggests that they figure they produced a genetic line up too good not to use twice?

A World after Money?

I'd like to finish with one last injected dream of our future, or at least that of North America. It felt like somewhere south of the Great Lakes. Maybe Chicago?

It started when I woke into lucid consciousness, seemingly alone. Inside of a saucer shaped plasma craft of the sort encountered in Tepoztlan Mexico and photographed by Contactee Carlos Diaz. I was somehow informed by present but non visible entities that the 6 orange-red light 'doors,' that encircled me inside the saucer rim, all opened into the same time frame in the future of the US, but in 6 different places geographically. 5 opened into cities. One opened into the woods. Would I like to take a peek into the future?

Feeling reasonably wary, I selected the door into the woods. So I could observe the prevalent culture from a remove, before exposing my presence.

My unseen companions seemed to approve of my caution.

I stepped through the red light, crouched and crawled out of a large hole under a root such as a small bear might make use of. Emerging into a park like setting.

Huge trees, obviously wild and untended, rose over a lightly landscaped under story. Yet something else looked

179

artificial. Scattered between the clusters of massive oaks stood the crumbled remains of building foundations, stone and brick. Almost swallowed in brush. They were everywhere, I realized. They didn't give the forest a creepy feeling, however. In fact the effect was peaceful and contemplative.

2 youngish men came into view, walking along a dirt path. They carried picks and shovels which struck me as very unfuturistic, and chatted amiably as they drew closer. It sounded like they had just finished rebuilding a footbridge and were on their way home.

I fell in behind them as they passed. And followed them a short way through the forest to come out in a clearing, containing a round kiosk, with trails radiating out from it like wheel spokes around a hub.

The men rested their tools against the building and chatted amiably with the lady inside the open window, who appeared to know them well. She reached into a drawer and gave each of them a small metal casting of a pickax, resembling a jewelry charm. They looked like cheap pot metal. This was their reward for their work on the bridge.

"Is that all they're paying you?" I blurted out, indignant for their sake.

They seemed to find my outburst amusing. "And what should they give us?" one inquired.

I discovered that no one was paid in what we called money anymore. Your basic life needs were provided by the the system as a whole, which was handled more like a locally owned grocery co-op then by the clunky style of government we use today.

One of them referred to it as the 'Natural Credit System'. Feeling my puzzlement he explained that he was joking. Actually the title was National Credit System.

You justified your keep, socially, by sequentially

volunteering for certain necessary jobs, according to your abilities and interests, after which you received a token charm as confirmation of your contribution. Some people kept and collected them like coins or stamps. But you didn't need to, it was all recorded. A day's work was about 4 hours on average. That gave you time for a garden or vocation of your own, for use in trade. Capitalism was still healthy, it appeared, just on a more local level.

Only ground level citizens comprised this Co Op government. No more presidents, no representatives, no Congress, no need. No Wall Street. Nearly everything operated at the neighborhood level now. The workers I spoke to sounded reasonably satisfied with the arrangement.

And the ruins, what happened? And when? Those were some tall oaks growing through them.

No it wasn't the result of any war, they explained. Just one reminder of the 'Hard Times'. Most people had moved to the country during a major economic depression. And had stripped away much of the urban building material, bricks and blocks for building their farm structures, leaving what resembled a conflict zone. Yet maybe because of the foliage which was steadily taking back the landscape, the atmosphere felt surprisingly ambient. I was standing in a park, set aside and maintained as a living reminder of the past.

And they still had something resembling money, as it turned out; though used mainly for convenience, trading out of the area. The 'coins' looked like plastic checkers or poker chips. They weren't used very much.

I woke up with the exhilarating conviction that I'd just been given a preview of a whole new future social system. One that actually seemed to function for the people and in such an egalitarian manner!

But when was the actual year I visited? And when were the 'Hard Times'? Now I wish I'd asked more questions---.

.

Valenya

Notes and Suggestions

If you enjoyed this book there's a pretty good chance you might also be interested in---

The research of Colin and Synthia Andrews, especially but not limited to the subject of crop circle science. My suggestion would be to start with the book 'Circular Evidence', by Colin; the very first in depth book on the phenomena. Then read the last book 'On the Edge of Reality' by Colin and Synthia to get an overview on their current focus.

The Path of Energy by Synthia (a naturopathic physician) reveals an energy science that may also tie in to the crop circle story. Government Circles by Colin proves that although intensely interested in the crop circles from the very beginning, the British Government has steadfastly lied about it. Now why would they do that?

The research of Kathleen Marden and Denise Stoner, especially in the fascinating area of Encounter Experience commonalities. Besides offering a comprehensive list, their book 'The Alien Abduction Files' also covers selected individual accounts in more depth then is usually given in most collections and the stories are much richer as a result.

I found the multiple abduction accounts to be especially interesting. In particular, that of the Reed family, whose group experience actually resulted in a commemorative plaque being erected to record the abduction as a confirmed historical event.

The research of T.R. Dutton as compiled and recounted in his book, 'UFOs in Reality'. Many UFO researchers are still unaware of his work in tracking the routes followed punctually by whatever UFOs might represent. Following a flurry in his home area of Southern England, he took early retirement from his position as a British Aerospace Engineer in order to study the phenomena in depth. Although he could never figure out how they flew---his original focus---he did happen to uncover a network of predictable 'track lines,' followed by UFOs once they'd entered Earth's orbit.

He could and did print out timetables for probable fly overs in any area you might request. Not only suggesting what time to expect them but even which horizon you should be facing. Since the track lines repeat every year, I've used my area's chart to unexpected success, when I realized he'd 'predicted' a fly over at the precise time I'd experienced a contact several years previous.

Also included in UFOs in Reality are some especially absorbing personal accounts of both UFO sightings and abductions researched by the author in person.

No, I don't get a kickback on suggesting any of these books. When you discover something interesting, you just want to share it.

Oh, and check out Ivan Sanderson. I know he passed some years ago but his work is still relevant, and his semi Fortean attitude and engaging conversational style makes his work such a pleasure to read. Besides covering 'big' subjects like Bigfoot, vortex patterns and UFOs, he also carried out impromptu ESP experiments with jungle ants. I collect his books, proudly possessing the classic Uninvited Visitors with the early proto holographic-style cover art of a hovering saucer, with grooves cut about as deeply as those of an old phonograph record. The gem of my collection, discovered in a thrift shop. Where all good books retire.

His buddy John Keel was pretty good too. And still is.

Reflections from a Crop Circle Case

Valenya

Valenya has always studied certain fringe sciences to a degree many would probably regard as obsessive. The fruits of her research have been featured in Fate, UFO Magazine, Lost Treasure Magazine and the Curly Horse Gazette.

She lives in the mountains of Oregon with her life mate Terry, 3 horses, 2 dogs and a cat, working as a crafts faire jeweler while creating block prints and studying Sumerian in her spare time.

Reflections from a Crop Circle Case

Proof

Made in the USA
Columbia, SC
27 July 2017